OFFICIAL COMPANION TO THE #1 WORLDWIDE BESTSELLER

THE
ATOMIC
HABITS
WORKBOOK

JAMES CLEAR

AVERY

an imprint of Penguin Random House

New York

THE
ATOMIC
HABITS
WORKBOOK

Simple Exercises for
Building the Life
You Want

A

AVERY

an imprint of Penguin Random House LLC
1745 Broadway, New York, NY 10019
penguinrandomhouse.com

Avery with colophon is a trademark of Penguin Random House LLC

Most Avery books are available at a discount when purchased in quantity for
sales promotions or corporate use. Special editions, which include personalized
covers, excerpts, and corporate imprints, can be created when purchased in large quantities.
For more information, please e-mail specialmarkets@penguinrandomhouse.com. Your local
bookstore can also assist with discounted bulk purchases using
the Penguin Random House corporate Business-to-Business program.
For assistance in locating a participating retailer,
e-mail B2B@penguinrandomhouse.com.

ISBN 9798217180509

Printed in the United States of America
1st Printing

The authorized representative in the EU for product safety and compliance is
Penguin Random House Ireland, Morrison Chambers, 32 Nassau Street,
Dublin D02 YH68, Ireland, https://eu-contact.penguin.ie.

Contents

PART II

The Four Laws of Behavior Change

PART III

Living with Your Habits:
Building a Mindset for Long-Term Success

TOOLBOX

Pain Point Index

QUICK HELP FOR SOME COMMON
HABIT-RELATED PROBLEMS

Introduction

A FEW YEARS AFTER *Atomic Habits* was published, I was speaking to a group of college coaches and athletic directors. After the talk, a man named Travis Wall came up to me and said that he had been the head coach of the men's soccer team at St. Olaf College in Minnesota.

"I read *Atomic Habits* soon after moving to Minnesota in the spring of 2019," he said. "I was inheriting a team that went 5–13 the year preceding and 4–13–1 the year before that. Your book helped me articulate the blueprint I wanted to have to help turn our program around."

He went on to explain the system he used to install better habits throughout the program. "The first preseason," he said, "we showed the team a presentation that was rooted in examples of little things we had to get better at. While we did explain the roles and responsibilities we'd have on the field, we also talked about things like breaking in new soccer cleats properly to not get blisters, wearing the appropriate gear on the correct day, how to take ice baths, etc. This was taken directly from the British Cycling team example in *Atomic Habits* and how they began their transformation by examining things like the mattresses they slept on, the comfort of their seat on their bike, and so on. They focused more on environmental changes versus cycling changes to start, and that is essentially how we started rebuilding the program."

He had my interest, and I asked for more information about his approach. He said, "This presentation became something we'd revisit annually when talking about the importance of having systems and doing our best to stick to them. We had systems for how we recruited, how we designed our training sessions, our feedback loops with our players. I don't think we would have had them had it not been for reading your book.

"Your quote 'We do not rise to the level of our goals, we fall to the level of our systems' has been ingrained in my mind since reading the book," Wall said.*

Here's what happened next:

2018: 5–13, ninth place in the conference
2019: 9–10, sixth place in the conference; first year under the new system
2020: Season canceled due to COVID-19
2021: 19–3–1, Conference Champions, NCAA Sweet 16
2022: 15–5–2, Conference Champions, NCAA Sweet 16
2023: 20–3–3, Conference Champions, NCAA National Champions

They went from five wins in 2018 to national champions five years later.

When I originally wrote *Atomic Habits*, I never could have imagined what it would go on to become. I'd hoped I had written a good book, of course, but I don't think any reasonable person could expect to sell twenty million copies in the first five years. *Atomic Habits* has become a phenomenon with a life of its own, and millions of readers around the world have now embraced the book's core message: Small changes compound into remarkable results.

The trajectory of your life bends in the direction of your habits. Whatever you repeat, you reinforce. And my readers continually remind me of the influence that habits can have on our lives.

---

* Conversation with Travis Wall at the NCAC Summit on May 20, 2024; Email exchange with Travis Wall on May 22, 2024.

I receive messages every day from people who share how *Atomic Habits* has transformed their health, relationships, and careers, and made them think differently about the profound power they have over their own lives. I hear from childhood friends who say that after reading *Atomic Habits*, they lost over a hundred pounds and stopped drinking. I read emails from therapists and psychologists who assign *Atomic Habits* as "homework" to their clients. I hear from surgeons who have changed how their teams prepare for operations. And I hear from countless parents, teachers, and coaches who share the concepts with their children, students, and players. I've even seen photos of *Atomic Habits* tattoos.

But even though these stories are incredible, the national championships and the weight-loss transformations and the tattoos aren't the things that really get me. What makes me tear up is when I hear about how differently people *feel* about themselves. The people who tell me their story and say, "My kids are proud of me." Or when a reader tells me, "*Atomic Habits* got me out of a dark place and helped me refocus my life." Or when someone says, "For the first time in many years, I can look in the mirror and feel good about who I am becoming." That stuff gets me because that's what it's always been about: using your habits as a method to develop into the type of person you want to be.

These stories remind me why I wrote the book in the first place, which is to help and empower others. To help people who feel stuck find a path toward actual, sustainable transformation. To empower people to feel like they are in the driver's seat of their lives. That's the purpose of this workbook too.

Readers love *Atomic Habits* (it's the highest-rated habits book of all time), but I've learned that people can always use more concrete help implementing new habits. The gap between understanding and doing is real and can be tough to bridge. You can read about the importance of environmental design, but redesigning your actual living room can feel overwhelming and complicated. You can learn about habit stacking, but actually taking the time to create effective habit stacks during busy mornings can feel daunting. You can understand the power of identity-based habits but feel stuck on how to begin crafting them. Sometimes everything sounds straightforward when you read about it, but you still need a nudge to get started.

That's where this workbook comes in. It breaks down the ideas and exercises from *Atomic Habits* into simple, actionable steps that anyone can perform. Instead of wondering how to apply the Four Laws of Behavior Change to your habits, you'll work through exercises that make the application obvious.

This workbook is intended as a companion to *Atomic Habits* and so works best when you use them together. But if you are using it on its own, or read *Atomic Habits* a while ago, don't worry. The workbook includes refreshers on the core ideas from the book, so you can use it without needing to reread the original text.

Part I begins with the section "The Science of Habit," a review of the most important ideas from *Atomic Habits*. Then you'll assess your current situation and needs so that you know both what you want to work on and what life factors you'll need to take into account. Part II, "The Four Laws of Behavior Change," walks you step-by-step through exercises to help you practice and integrate these principles as you build and break habits. Once you've mastered the four laws, Part III, "Living with Your Habits," helps you build a mindset that can support your habits for the long run. Finally, the "Toolbox" contains a habit quick-start guide, a one-page summary of key ideas, "cheat sheets" for building and breaking habits, and a habit tracker.

As you work through the book, you'll notice that there are not separate sections for building and breaking habits. I wrote it this way for the simple reason that strategies for building and breaking habits are usually two sides of the same coin. With a little tweaking, most exercises can be used for both. If you find yourself leaning toward focusing only on good habits (or only on breaking bad ones), that's fine. Use the workbook in whatever way is best for you.

HOW TO GET THE MOST OUT OF THIS WORKBOOK

When contemplating behavior change, I know—from talking with readers and from my own life—that the impulse to try to change everything at once is strong. But my goal is to help you approach behavior change in the way that sets you up for success. For this reason, I've provided space to work through each exercise for two habits. My recommendation is that you work on only one habit at a time, but I've given space for two in case you want to work through the book a second time with a different habit—or you have two in mind you want to tackle right away.

The piece that is harder for me to help you with is your expectations around timing. Mastery requires both impatience and patience. The impatience to have a bias toward action, to not waste time, and to work with a sense of urgency each day. The patience to delay gratification, to wait for your actions to accumulate, and to trust the process. This workbook is designed to help you do both: practice the things today that will pay off in the long run. If I do my job well, then these exercises will help you take more time to carefully build a habit—and stick with it longer—than you might otherwise.

Which brings me to my final point on how to get the most out of this workbook. There is no single way to build better habits; there are many. My approach is to empower, not to prescribe. A habit that may be additive to one person may be detrimental to another, and a habit-building strategy that may work well for a friend may be useless to you. I'm not interested in telling you which habits you should build or which choices you should make. Instead, I want to equip and empower you with ideas and strategies so you can make your own choices and do the things you want to do.

That's why there are many strategies here. The intention is not that you ultimately adopt each one—I don't care if you skip half the exercises in this book—but what I hope is that you come away feeling like you have a whole toolbox of options to choose from and that you find the tools that are right for you. Take what works for you, and leave the rest.

HOW TO GET STARTED

If there's one piece of wisdom I'd like to leave with you, it's this: Always work with your life. Life is dynamic, not static. What works for you will likely shift over time. We are always evolving, which means that a habit or strategy that once worked well for you may no longer make sense.

Certain life changes, like moving cities, entering a relationship, starting a new job, having a child, and so on, can radically change the shape of your life, making old habits obsolete. Don't be a prisoner to your past habits. Instead of spending your energy trying to force old habits, use it to form new ones that actually fit the current shape of your life.

One of my favorite sayings is "Don't rush, but don't wait." We all have things we hope to achieve with our lives. If there is something you wish to do, go do it. Death comes for busy people too. It will not pause and return at a more convenient time. The timing rarely seems perfect. Accept your current moment, develop a willingness to adapt, and take the first small step forward.

Today might be the best chance you have to take action. The longer you wait, the more deeply embedded you get in your current lifestyle. Your habits solidify. Your beliefs harden. You get comfortable. It will never be easy, but it may also never be easier than it is right now. When you procrastinate on something important, you are choosing to delay a better future.

This workbook is where that transformation begins. Let's get started.

—*James Clear, 2025*

PART I

Foundations

It's remarkable what you can build if you just don't stop.

THE SCIENCE OF HABIT
A Brief Overview of the Theory of Behavior Change

BEFORE WE START practicing behavior change, let's take a moment to review the key concepts you need in order to understand the theory behind it. If you've just come from reading *Atomic Habits*, feel free to skip right to "Habit Assessment," but if it's been a while or you want a refresher, read on. Everything else we will discuss in this workbook is built on these principles, so understanding them is crucial.

1 PERCENT BETTER EVERY DAY

The typical approach to self-improvement is to set a large goal, then try to take big leaps in order to accomplish it in as little time as possible. Too often, we convince ourselves that change is meaningful only if there is some large, visible outcome associated with it. Whether it is getting stronger, building a business, traveling the world, or any number of goals, we put pressure on ourselves to make some earth-shattering improvement that will awe everyone around us.

Success is the product of daily habits—not once-in-a-lifetime transformations.

While this may sound good in theory, it often ends in burnout, frustration, and failure. And yet, while improving by just 1 percent every day isn't notable (and sometimes isn't even *noticeable*), it can be just as meaningful, especially in the long run.

It is so easy to dismiss the value of making slightly better decisions on a daily basis. Sticking with the fundamentals is not impressive. Falling in love with boredom is not exciting. Getting 1 percent better isn't going to make headlines.

There is one thing about it though: It works.

In the beginning, there is basically no difference between making a choice that is 1 percent better or not. (In other words, it won't impact you very much today.) But as time goes on, these small improvements compound, and you suddenly find a very big gap between people who make slightly better decisions on a daily basis and those who don't.

Here's the punch line: If you get 1 percent better each day for one year, you'll end up thirty-seven times better by the time you're done. That's probably a more massive result than you would ever expect, even from a onetime heroic leap, and yet it's achievable through just one tiny change a day.

1 PERCENT BETTER EVERY DAY

1 percent worse every day for one year. $0.99^{365} = 00.03$
1 percent better every day for one year. $1.01^{365} = 37.78$

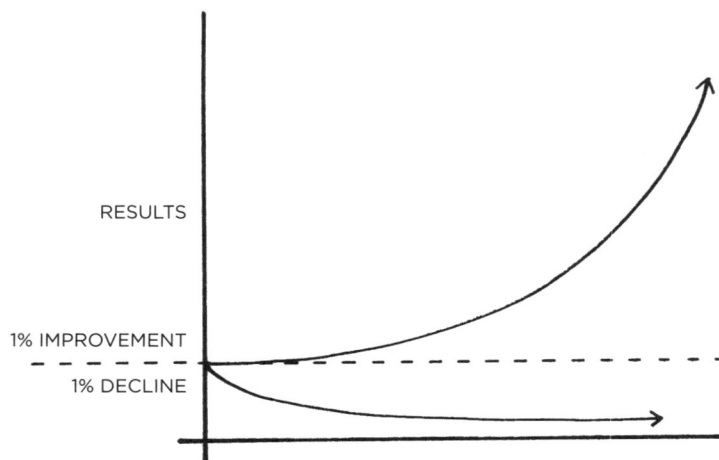

This is why small choices don't make much of a difference at the time but add up over the long term.

But here's the thing: If positive compounding is true, then so is the inverse. If you get 1 percent *worse* each day for one year, you'll decline nearly down to zero. The lesson is that what starts as a small win, or a minor setback, grows into something much greater.

This is why the first important concept when it comes to behavior change is the key role of continuous self-improvement. Just one tiny shift can change everything. If you want to predict where you'll end up in life, all you have to do is follow the curve of tiny gains and losses and see how your daily choices will compound ten or twenty years down the line.

This is why it doesn't matter how successful or unsuccessful you are right now. What matters is whether your habits are putting you on the path toward success. Focus on your current trajectory, not your current results. It's a much better indicator of where you're headed.

So stop obsessing over the big and start focusing on the small—it's the key to building the life you want.

Time magnifies the margin between success and failure.

It will multiply whatever you feed it. Good habits make

time your ally. Bad habits make time your enemy.

THE PLATEAU OF LATENT POTENTIAL

One crucial thing to understand about compounding change is that exponential growth happens in a way that can be hard for us to wrap our minds around. When we make changes, our brains expect a linear upward progression, where we see consistent improvement the whole time. This is what's attractive about big change: immediate results. When we make change this way, the initial phases can feel amazing. That is, until you inevitably burn out and abandon the project.

Change can take years—before it happens all at once. Mastery requires patience.

But when improving by 1 percent a day, the opposite is true. Since the initial changes are so small, it can take a while before the effects become visible. This can lead to a period that I call the *Valley of Disappointment*, when your results lag behind your expectations. A few weeks or months of 1 percent improvement may not feel like they yield much, and that can be discouraging and lead people to give up. But if you haven't seen improvement yet, it's not because it isn't happening; it's because it just hasn't passed the threshold of visibility yet. I call that threshold the *Plateau of Latent Potential*, and it's the moment when your results and your expectations finally align and you start seeing change.

THE PLATEAU OF LATENT POTENTIAL

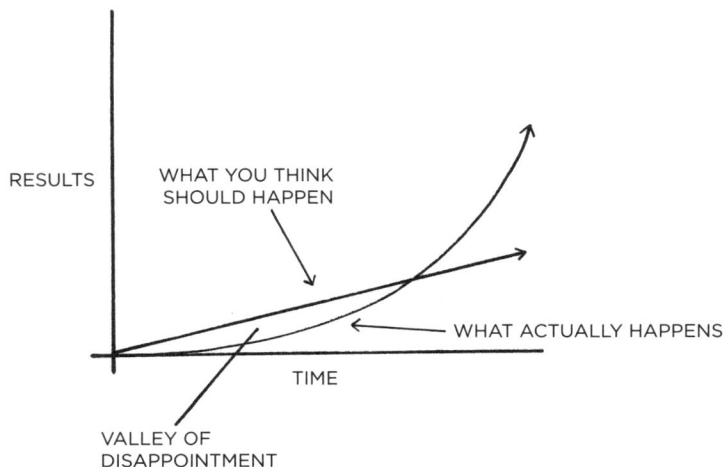

RESULTS

WHAT YOU THINK SHOULD HAPPEN

WHAT ACTUALLY HAPPENS

TIME

VALLEY OF DISAPPOINTMENT

The good news is that after you pass the plateau, it can feel like change happens in a big way all at once. All the work you've put in finally comes to fruition, and the ultimate outcome can exceed even your wildest expectations.

As you start a journey of continuous improvement, remember that change is happening even if you don't see it. The key is to just stick with it long enough to actually reap your results. Be patient and give yourself time to cross the plateau.

When you finally break through the Plateau of Latent Potential, people will call it an overnight success. The outside world only sees the most dramatic event rather than all that preceded it. But you know that it's the work you did long ago—when it seemed that you weren't making any progress—that makes the jump today possible.

SYSTEMS OVER GOALS

Another mistake people make when they try to change their habits is to go about it by trying to achieve a goal. You'll hear this strategy touted in many contexts, from school to business to the gym: If you want to achieve success, set specific, actionable goals and keep your sights on them.

> *Goals are best for people who care about winning once; systems are best for people who care about winning repeatedly.*

The problem with this is that it doesn't work. Why? Because results have very little to do with your goals and nearly everything to do with your systems.

Goals are the results you want to achieve; systems are the processes that lead to those results. It's hard to have success if you focus only on your end goal and not on *how* you're going to get there. Does this mean that goals are useless? Not at all! Goals are good for setting a direction, but systems are necessary for actually making progress. Trying to achieve a *new* goal with the *same* system you've been using is useless. The same system will always lead you to the same goal. Which means that if you want to achieve a new goal, you need to design a new system for getting there. You do not rise to the level of your goals. You fall to the level of your systems.

If you're having trouble changing your habits, the problem isn't you or a lack of motivation. The problem is your system. Bad habits repeat themselves again and again not because you don't want to change, but because you have the wrong system for change. Change the system and change your life.

When you fall in love with the process rather than the product, you don't have to wait to give yourself permission to be happy. You can be satisfied any time your system is running.

IDENTITY-BASED HABITS

The other problem with focusing on a goal is that approaching change that way is exceedingly difficult. There are two reasons for this: (1) It does not provide a process for how to get there (as just discussed), and (2) it does not take into account how psychology actually works.

Stop worrying about results and start worrying about your identity. Become the type of person who can achieve the things you want to achieve.

Fundamentally, our behaviors are the most outward expression of our innermost identity—our values, our beliefs, how we see ourselves. If you see yourself as a runner, chances are you regularly run. If you see yourself as a musician, chances are that you spend time practicing an instrument. If you see yourself as a self-starter, chances are that you're quite proactive. When we identify a certain way, performing the behaviors that align with this identity comes easily. After all, they don't feel like effort, they just feel like being who we are. The behaviors that feel like a chore are the ones that are incongruent with your identity: saving money even though you identify as someone who loves shopping, saying no to a cigarette even though you identify as a smoker. These actions feel hard because they feel like something we are *trying* to do instead of something that we naturally are. Good habits can make rational sense, but if they conflict with your identity, you will fail to put them into action.

This is why the key to building lasting habits is focusing on creating a new identity first. Your current behaviors are simply a reflection of your current identity. True behavior change is identity change. You might start a habit because of motivation, but the only reason you'll stick with one is that it becomes part of your identity. To change your behavior for good, you need to start believing new things about yourself.

If you see yourself as a nail biter, trying not to bite your nails is going to feel difficult—it will feel at odds with who you are. But if you try to see yourself as someone who *doesn't* bite their nails, the behavior change won't feel so difficult after all.

The connection between identity and action is a feedback loop. The more you reframe your identity to align with your goals ("I'm not a nail biter—I'm someone who takes care of their hands"), the more likely it is that you will be able to perform those behaviors. At the same time, the more you perform the habits associated with a certain identity, the more you will inhabit that identity.

So how do you actually put this into practice? It's a two-step process:

1. Decide the type of person you want to be.
2. Prove it to yourself with small wins.

Decide who you want to be, and then work backward from there, thinking about the behaviors that kind of person performs. Then start performing those behaviors. Every action you take is a vote for the type of person you wish to become. The more you act like the identity you're trying to embody, the more you will feel like you inhabit that identity, and the easier it will be to keep acting that way. It's a flywheel that becomes easier every time.

This is the real reason why habits matter. Not because they help you achieve certain things, but because they help you become the person you wish to be. Focus on *who* you want to be, not *what* you want to do—it is the surest way to create a life you love.

The process of building habits is actually

the process of becoming yourself.

THE HABIT LOOP

A habit is an automatic behavior that has been formed by your brain encoding a feedback loop. Whenever you encounter a new problem in your life, your brain tries out a solution for it. If the attempted solution doesn't work, your brain sees it as a failure, and nothing is encoded. But if the attempted solution results in something positive—a reward—your brain takes note of the behavior that led there. The next time you face the same problem, your brain will try out the solution that worked before, and if it again results in a reward, the solution will be further enforced. And if you face the problem repeatedly, your brain will automate the process of solving it. That's what your habits are: a series of automatic solutions that solve the problems and stresses you face regularly.

This automatic nature is why, once a habit has formed, we do it without even thinking about it, which is incredibly powerful. It means that you can perform a habit on automatic without expending your brain's precious and limited energy consciously thinking about it. Habits are energy savers, reducing cognitive load and freeing up mental capacity for other tasks. Building habits in the present allows you to do more of what you want in the future. But this automatic nature also means that once they *are* formed, they can be incredibly difficult to break.

So how do habits form, and how do they break?

The process of building a habit can be divided into four simple steps: cue, craving, response, and reward. This four-step pattern is the backbone of every habit, and your brain runs through these steps in the same order each time.

Cue—The thing that triggers your brain to initiate the behavior. It is the piece of information that indicates that a reward might be nearby.

Craving—The motivational force behind every habit. It is the desire for something about your internal state to be changed, and it is how your mind interprets the cue, transforming it from just a sound or sight into a problem to be solved.

Response—The actual habit that you perform, which can take the form of a thought or an action. The response is the actual *solution* to the problem.

Reward—The end goal of every habit, the thing you hoped to achieve by performing the behavior in the first place.

The cue is about noticing the reward. The craving is about wanting the reward. The response is about obtaining the reward. The reward satisfies us and teaches us that performing this behavior results in the reward. Together, these four steps form a neurological feedback loop that allows you to create automatic habits. This cycle is known as the *habit loop*.

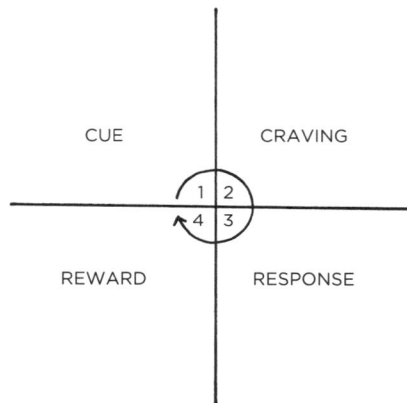

CUE   CRAVING

1 | 2
4 | 3

REWARD   RESPONSE

To see what this looks like in your own life, take a few habits—a couple positive and a couple negative—that you repeat every day, and for each one, identify the cue, craving, response, and reward. Because habits are automatic, identifying these components can be trickier than you might expect. But learning this skill is crucial to breaking existing habits and building strong new ones.

Habit: _____

Cue	Craving
1	2
4	3
Reward	**Response**

Habit: _____

Cue	Craving
1	2
4	3
Reward	**Response**

Habit: _____

Cue	Craving
1	2
4	3
Reward	**Response**

Habit: _____

Cue	Craving
1	2
4	3
Reward	**Response**

THE FOUR LAWS OF BEHAVIOR CHANGE

The habit loop teaches us how to understand our habits, but not necessarily how to actually go about building and breaking them. For that, we need the *Four Laws of Behavior Change,* which turn the four steps of habit building into a simple set of rules for creating good habits and breaking bad ones. The laws show us how to build good habits, and the inverted laws show us how to break bad ones. You can think of each law as a lever that influences human behavior. When the levers are in the right positions, creating good habits is effortless. When they are in the wrong positions, it is nearly impossible. Here they are:

The Habit Loop	THE FOUR LAWS OF BEHAVIOR CHANGE	
	Building Good Habits	Breaking Bad Habits
1. Cue	The First Law: *Make It Obvious*	The First Law Inverted: *Make It Invisible*
2. Craving	The Second Law: *Make It Attractive*	The Second Law Inverted: *Make It Unattractive*
3. Response	The Third Law: *Make It Easy*	The Third Law Inverted: *Make It Difficult*
4. Reward	The Fourth Law: *Make It Satisfying*	The Fourth Law Inverted: *Make It Unsatisfying*

The four laws are how we take the theory that we have been reviewing and make it practical, turning it from an idea into something we can actually use to change the course of our lives.

For the rest of this workbook, after taking a moment to assess our habit landscape, we will focus on the four laws. We will dig into them in detail, practicing how we can use them to build good habits and break bad ones.

HABIT ASSESSMENT
Understanding Your Current Landscape and Planning for Success

THE POWER OF ASSESSMENT

Before you begin changing your habits, it's critical to start with an assessment. This isn't the most exciting part of the process—I get it. When you're motivated to change, you want to jump straight into action. You want to start the new morning routine, download the meditation app, or get the gym membership. But here's the thing: It does you no good to change before we understand what needs changing.

Assessment is necessary to ensure two fundamental things: that you're solving the right problem and that you're solving it the right way. It's remarkable how easy it is to spend months of effort optimizing for the wrong behavior or chasing a goal that doesn't actually align with the life you want to build. Without assessment, we default to assumptions, and our assumptions are often wrong.

In this section, we'll disrupt that pattern by starting from a place of awareness. Assessment creates clarity. It reveals the hidden patterns that govern your days, exposes the false assumptions that have been holding you back, and highlights opportunities you might otherwise miss. Most important, it ensures that when you do decide to climb, you're scaling the right mountain.

To do this effectively, we'll use what I call the *ABZ* framework. *A* represents an honest assessment of your current reality, not where you think you are or wish you were. *Z* represents where you want to end up—the person you want to become and the life you want to live. *B* through *Y* are the steps that it takes to get from *A* to *Z*. Here's the key insight: Most people think that to get from *A* to *Z*, they need to map out every step from *B* through *Y*. But that's not true. You only need to know *B*. The path to *Z* is just a series of *B*'s, one after another.

In this section, we will start by tackling *A* and *Z*, assessing your current reality without judgment and determining where you want to go. By the end, you'll be able to define *B*—the next right step—which is the habit we'll spend the rest of this workbook mastering. Each section will provide a number of strategies for exploring each element, with the hope that some will resonate. Don't worry if not everything works for you—focus on what you find most useful.

Remember, all you need to do to get to *Z* is repeat *B* again and again. One small step, then another, then another. That's how mountains are climbed and lives are transformed.

YOUR CURRENT REALITY

Success is not a goal to reach or a finish line to cross.

It is a system to improve, an endless process to refine.

The Big Picture

How would you rate your current level of contentment with your personal and professional life and why?

Personal

| 1 | 2 | 3 | 4 | 5 |

Why?_____

_____

_____

_____

Professional

| 1 | 2 | 3 | 4 | 5 |

Why?_____

_____

_____

_____

What are your top three priorities at the moment?

1. _____

_____

_____

2. _____

_____

_____

3. _____

_____

_____

_____

What are you optimizing for right now?

_____

_____

_____

_____

What major projects are you working on? How is each going?

Project	How It's Going

What are the nonnegotiable obligations in your life right now?

- _____

- _____

- _____

- _____

- _____

What is working well in your life and what isn't?

Working Well	Not Working Well

What are the things that keep holding you back, and how could you overcome them?

_____

_____

_____

_____

_____

_____

What are the major things you know you would like to change in your life, and why?

_____

_____

_____

_____

_____

_____

Time and Energy Audit

We often think that every hour in the day has equal potential. If we are awake for sixteen hours a day, we tell ourselves that we have sixteen hours to use for all the things we want to accomplish. But this isn't the case. Subtract the hours necessary for taking care of our basic needs, daily responsibilities, and the lag time around activities, and we are left with far fewer. Acknowledge that in the remaining hours, your energy and focus are high for only a fraction of the time, and we are left with fewer still.

The truth is that each of us has only two to six high-quality hours every day. Understanding which these are for you is crucial to using them wisely, especially when it comes to supporting your habits. Build habits that work with your time and energy levels, and you set yourself up for success. Building habits that don't is a recipe for failure.

Optimizing your time is not about figuring out how to use *more* hours in a day—it's about figuring out how to maximize the ones you already have.

Let's start by taking an audit of your time and energy. Over the course of the next week, for each hour in the day that you are awake, (1) jot down a one-word description of what you were doing (for example, "cooking"), and (2) mark (↑ , —, ↓) how

Time	Mon	Tues	Weds	Thurs	Fri	Sat	Sun
4 a.m.							
5 a.m.							
6 a.m.							
7 a.m.							
8 a.m.							
9 a.m.							
10 a.m.							
11 a.m.							
12 p.m.							
1 p.m.							
2 p.m.							
3 p.m.							

high your energy levels felt. This is how you determine your best hours. Note: Capture your week as it is, don't try to increase productivity. Accuracy is key.

Time	Mon	Tues	Weds	Thurs	Fri	Sat	Sun
4 p.m.							
5 p.m.							
6 p.m.							
7 p.m.							
8 p.m.							
9 p.m.							
10 p.m.							
11 p.m.							
12 a.m.							
1 a.m.							
2 a.m.							
3 a.m.							

Look at the grid and note the patterns you're seeing.

What are the major ways that you're spending your time right now?

- _____

- _____

- _____

- _____

- _____

How many good, high-quality, high-energy hours do you have a day? Which are they?

_____

_____

_____

What activities are currently getting these best hours?

_____

_____

_____

_____

What are your lowest-energy hours a day?

_____

_____

_____

_____

What do you want to get done in your best hours versus your leftover hours?

Best	Leftover
_____	_____
_____	_____
_____	_____
_____	_____
_____	_____
_____	_____
_____	_____

Now let's think big picture. What feels like it's consuming more of your attention or time than it should?

_____

_____

_____

_____

_____

What's currently your biggest source of stress or mental energy drain?

_____

_____

_____

_____

_____

_____

_____

Change is hard, and trying to make too much change at once is a recipe for burnout. Before you embark on changing your habits, what kinds of significant changes or transitions are you already navigating or anticipating navigating soon? Being aware of this can help you decide what additional changes make the most sense for you to take on right now.

_____

_____

_____

_____

_____

_____

_____

Past Attempts

When designing habits for the future, one of the most powerful tools is our past track record. Looking at what's worked and what hasn't is incredibly useful data for making future plans.

First, think about the most beneficial habits you've had—or currently have—in your life. Write them below, along with what's made them have a positive impact.

Habit	Why It's Positive

Now consider your past or current habits again, but this time think about the ones that you have been the most successful at sticking with. Write the habits below, along with why you think they've stuck in your life.

Habit	Why It's Sticky

Looking at your past data, reflect on what has made habits positive and sticky in your life. What patterns are you seeing, and what can you learn from these?

_____

_____

_____

_____

_____

_____

_____

Now let's look at your attempts at building and breaking habits. Below, list recent or notable attempts at behavior change that you see as successful. Try to think of some for building and some for breaking. For each, note what worked well.

Habit	Building/Breaking	What Worked

Do the same exercise, but think about what hasn't worked. For each attempt, list what didn't work, and then whether this obstacle was internal or external.

Habit	Building/Breaking	What Didn't Work	Internal/External Obstacle

Looking at your past data, reflect on what has and hasn't worked for you when it comes to behavior change. What patterns are you seeing, and what can you learn from these?

_____

_____

_____

_____

_____

_____

Current Habit Inventory

It's time to take a detailed look at what your actual habit landscape looks like. While you may think that you have a good sense of the habits you perform on a daily basis, the automatic nature of habits means that we're often less aware of them than we think. One of the most powerful tools for making our habits more visible is also the simplest: the Habits Scorecard.

On the following pages are three scorecards: one for your morning routine, one for evening, and an additional one for another time in your day when your routine feels significant. For each, fill out the first column of the scorecard *while* you are doing your routine, noting everything that you do.

Afterward, go through and mark each habit as positive (+), neutral (=), or negative (–), according to whether each habit will benefit you in the long run. Then explain your reasoning for why you scored it that way. Remember, the goal of this isn't judgment, just increasing awareness of your behaviors.

MORNING SCORECARD

Habit	Score (+ / = / −)	Score Reasoning

What are your takeaways? Any habits that you want to remove or change? Anything that you would like to add?

_____

_____

_____

_____

_____

EVENING SCORECARD

Habit	Score (+ / = / −)	Score Reasoning

What are your takeaways? Any habits that you want to remove or change? Anything that you would like to add?

_____

_____

_____

_____

_____

ADDITIONAL SCORECARD

While mornings and evenings are times during the day when most of us have set routines, we often have other times during the day or week that are guided by routine as well. Is there another time when you think it would be helpful to reflect on your routine? Maybe right when you get home from work, or on Sunday afternoons when you're preparing for the week ahead? If so, use the scorecard below to score this routine.

Time: _____

Habit	Score (+ / = / −)	Score Reasoning

What are your takeaways? Any habits that you want to remove or change? Anything that you would like to add?

_____

_____

_____

_____

_____

_____

_____

Reflect

Now look back over the answers from this past section. What patterns do you see emerging? How would you sum up your current starting point? What's working, what isn't, and what parameters do you need to consider as you go forward with making changes?

_____

_____

_____

_____

_____

_____

_____

_____

WHERE YOU WANT TO END UP

Clarity is freedom. Know what is important to you and it will grant you the freedom to ignore everything else.

Clean Slate

When imagining where we want to end up, we often assume our current life and commitments are a given and work from there. The trouble with this is that time is a limited resource, and if you never reconsider these commitments, there will never be room for the larger changes that might be necessary.

What if you took the opposite approach? For this exercise, clear the slate. Instead of assuming your current commitments and responsibilities, start from square one. If you were building up your life from scratch, what would you want it to look like? The goal of this isn't to say that you don't need to work within your realities, but rather to let yourself imagine the life you want without feeling limited by your current obligations. In the ideating phase, prematurely limiting yourself only prevents you from discovering what you want.

First, what commitments would you have? Feel free to list both commitments you already have and those you would like to have, but make sure you add in only things you actually want.

- _____

- _____

- _____

- _____

- _____

- _____

- _____

Next, what commitments would you *not* have? Thinking about what you don't want to spend your time on can be even more important than thinking about what you do want to spend it on.

- _____

- _____

- _____

- _____

- _____

- _____

- _____

- _____

When you say no, you are only saying no to one option. When you say yes, you are saying no to every other option. No is a decision. Yes is a responsibility. Be careful what (and who) you say yes to. It will shape your day, your career, your family, your life.

Now think about how you want to spend your time. Below, picture your ideal day. What would it look like? How would you use the time? If it's helpful, think about the insights you surfaced during the Time and Energy Audit.

Morning	
Afternoon	
Evening	

Look at the answers on the previous page and reflect on what you learned from these exercises. What did you learn about what you want your life to contain? What did you learn about what you *don't* want your life to contain?

_____

_____

_____

_____

_____

_____

_____

_____

_____

_____

_____

_____

_____

_____

_____

_____

Your Ideal Future

Now let yourself dream big. What are the major goals you're coming into this process with?

- _____

- _____

- _____

- _____

- _____

- _____

We often think of our goals as occurring at a vague point in the future, but thinking in specific timelines can help you clarify. What do you hope your life looks like . . .

Six Months from Now	Two Years from Now	Ten Years from Now

Since goal setting and behavior change are ultimately about change, what are the major changes you would like to see in your life?

- _____

- _____

- _____

- _____

- _____

- _____

Success is a word that we throw around a lot, but it can mean radically different things to different people. Defining it for yourself is crucial to reaching it. What does *success* mean to you?

_____

_____

_____

_____

_____

_____

When we look to set goals for ourselves, we often default to setting career or financial goals, but there are so many other areas of life to think about. Below, write out your vision for how you want each domain in your life to look. Not all these areas are important in each of our lives, and that's OK.

Physical Well-Being	Mental Health	Career

Relationships & Social Connection	Learning	Financial Security & Freedom

Recreation & Fun	Creativity	Community & Contribution

Spirituality	Family	Legacy

Your Ideal Identity

Another way to figure out where you want to end up is through the idea of identity-based habits. Instead of thinking of goals for yourself and envisioning your ideal future, envision your ideal self. *Who* do you hope to be?

1. In the diagrams, list out the identities that you would most like to inhabit in the center circles. They can be ones that you already feel describe you, or they can be new ones. If you feel stuck, consider the domains of life that we worked with before.

2. Then, for each identity that you listed, consider, "What does that person do?" Brainstorm the habits or actions that support the identity, and write them in the outer circles.

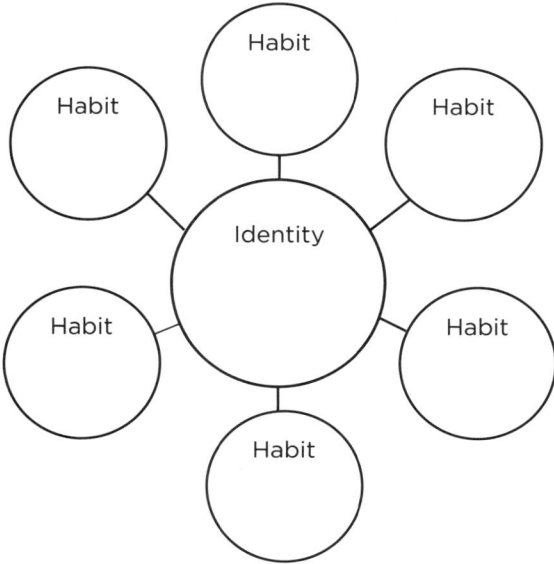
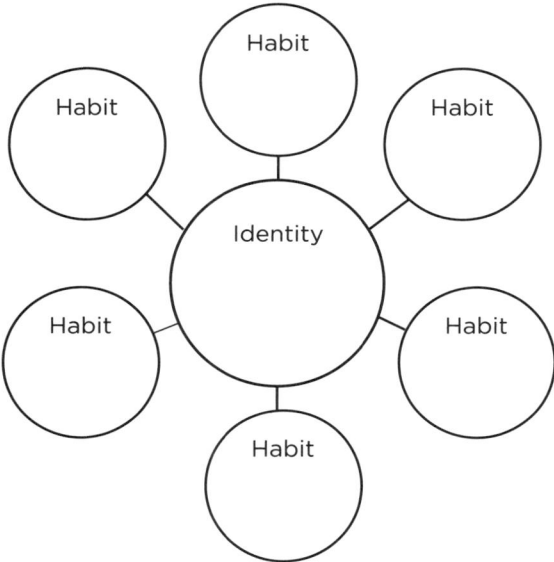
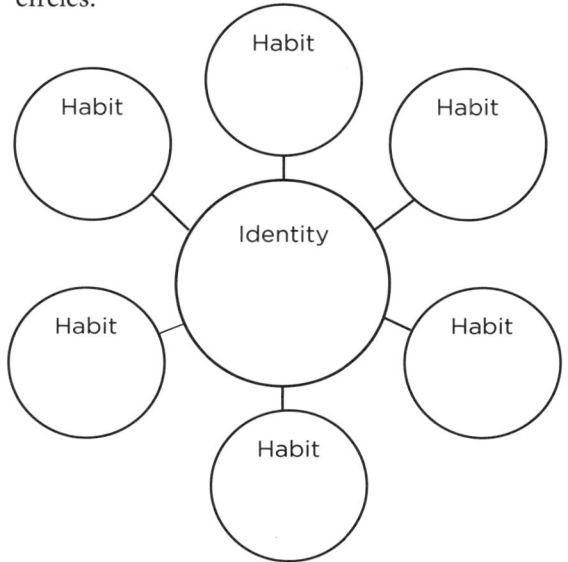

Goal Setting

Now look at the different exercises you've used to envision where you want to end up. What patterns are you seeing in what you brainstormed? What are you learning about what you want out of life and where you want to end up? What *don't* you want?

_____

_____

_____

_____

_____

_____

_____

_____

_____

_____

_____

_____

_____

Finally, based on the exercises you just completed, list out your concrete goals for yourself at this moment in time. At this stage, it's OK if they're big picture. We'll work on turning them into actionable systems next.

- _____

  _____

- _____

  _____

- _____

  _____

- _____

  _____

> *People will work for years and ultimately achieve a lifestyle that isn't quite what they were hoping for—often simply because they never clearly defined what they wanted. An hour of thinking can save you a decade of work.*

THE NEXT STEP

Just start. Start slow if you have to. Start small if you have to. Start privately if you have to. Just start.

Goals → Systems

Now that we've looked at where you're starting from (*A*) and where you want to end up (*Z*), it's time to figure out the next step (*B*). But how do we go about doing this? The answer lies in realizing that when we're talking about defining *B*, what we're really talking about is defining a system.

In "The Science of Habit," we discussed the importance of systems, and that while goals can be helpful for setting direction, when it comes to actually achieving your goals, the system is what's crucial. The key to the *ABZ* framework is understanding that it's saying the same thing. If *Z* is your goal, *B* is the first step of the system you will use to get there, and *A* supplies the facts about your reality that are needed to build a system that works for you. In other words, if *Z* is your goal, *B* is the habit you will focus on first in order to achieve it.

So, let's think about how to turn your goals into systems—and habits—that you can focus on building.

1. Start by again listing out the goals that you identified at the end of the "Where You Want to End Up" section.

2. For each goal, if it is a goal that you had coming into this process, write out what your current system is for achieving that goal. If you don't currently have a system, write "none."

Goal	Current System
1:	
2:	
3:	
4:	

3. For each goal, evaluate your system. Write why you think it's working or not (or both). Then rate the effectiveness of each system.

Goal	System Evaluation	Effectiveness Rating
1:		1 2 3 4 5
2:		1 2 3 4 5
3:		1 2 3 4 5
4:		1 2 3 4 5

4. For each goal, determine what you think the ideal system is. In order to design your system, look at both your evaluation of the current system and at the work you did in the section "Your Current Reality." Think about not just what the ideal system is, but what the ideal system is for *you*.

5. Break down each system into its individual component habits.

Goal	System	Habits
1:		
2:		
3:		
4:		

Choose Your Habit

You have now done the work needed to choose the habit you want to focus on. It can be a habit you're trying to build or one that you're trying to break, or a combination of the two, such as if you're trying to replace a habit with a different one.

When looking to make a change, my strong recommendation is always to only work on *one* habit at a time. This can be difficult to accept. It can be tempting to work on many at once, especially when you've just done the work to surface a lot of areas of desired change in your life. But the more change you try to make at once, the less successful you will be. So choose one habit, and once it is in place, come back to select your next habit to work on. It is for this reason that I have given room in the book to fill out most exercises twice—so that once you have completed one habit, you can go back and work through the exercises again with another habit.

There are two caveats to this. The first is that if you really must, it is possible to work on two habits at once as long as one is in your personal life and one is in your professional life. The two areas of life are often separate enough that it's manageable to work on behavior change in both without overwhelming yourself.

The second caveat is that you are allowed to change the habits you're working on over time. Committing to a habit doesn't mean that, no matter what, you must stay with this habit until it's fully integrated in your life. For a variety of reasons, you may begin the process and then decide that this habit isn't right for you. Maybe you decide that the habit isn't actually benefiting you, or perhaps you decide that it's not the best way to address your goal. In these cases, you should feel no guilt in switching to work on a different habit. The most important thing always is to work on the thing that works best for you. So if at any point while using this workbook you decide that changing your habit is beneficial, you may.

Which habit(s) will you work on?

Habit: _____

Habit: _____

Double Checks

Before you start work on your habit, there are two important tests to do on the one you've chosen. If your habit doesn't pass these, it won't help you and it won't work.

1. Will It Solve the Problem at the Branch or Root Level?

The first is to double-check that your chosen habit is actually solving the problem you want it to solve. All habits are solutions to a problem you face in your life. But if you embark on behavior change only to realize that the new behavior does not actually solve the problem, then it doesn't matter how effective you are at building your new habit—the problem will still go unsolved.

A helpful way to think about this is that all problems can be solved at the branch level or the root level. Remove the branches of a thornbush today and you'll avoid a scrape this year. But next year, you'll face the same problem again. Remove the root of the bush today, and the entire plant will die. For example, say you want to solve the problem of how you keep scrolling on your phone before bed. A branch-level solution is to take a melatonin and hope you'll get sleepy enough that you stop scrolling at a good hour. A root-level solution is to keep your phone out of your room while you sleep.

So, is your habit solving the problem at the branch level or the root level?

Below, for the habit you've chosen, list out the problem that it's solving, and then explain whether the habit is solving the problem at the branch or root level.

Habit	Problem It's Solving	Branch/Root Level

If you've discovered that your habit is solving the problem at the branch level, select a new habit that will solve the problem at the root level.

Habit: _____

Habit: _____

2. Will It Fit the Shape of Your Life?

The second important check is to make sure that the habit you've chosen works *with* the shape of your life. If you've decided you want to begin exercising more but have chosen to work out in the morning, when you're also responsible for childcare, that isn't setting yourself up for success.

One particular thing worth calling out here is the tendency to want to make change by returning to old habits. How many times have you heard a friend say a version of "I just need to start running again," or "If only I could get back to the morning routine I used to have." This way of thinking is understandable—change is hard, and turning to something that's worked in the past can seem like obvious, low-hanging fruit.

The problem is that life inevitably changes, and if you're trying to return to a habit that belonged to an earlier version of your life, you may find that the habit no longer works for you. In fact, the reason that you no longer perform this habit is likely that it stopped working for your life. Trying to force the habit again can be discouraging and lead to you abandoning the habit altogether.

The solution is to acknowledge the change, and then consider what shape your habits need to take for your current life. You can spend your time wishing that the habit still fit, or you can use the time to design a habit that actually works for your life now. Only one leads to you making the change you desire.

On the next page, for the habit(s) you've chosen, write out how it takes into account the shape of your current life. To do this, flip back to the section "Your Current Reality" to see what you surfaced about what your life looks like right now.

Habit	How It Takes Into Account Your Life

If you've discovered that your habit doesn't take into account the current shape of your life, select a new habit that will.

Habit: _____

Habit: _____

Committing to Your Habit

When you're looking to make a change, one of the best things you can do to make the change stick is to commit. As we will discuss later, commitment-keeping devices are a particularly powerful version of this, but any commitment you make—even if it's just to yourself—can be helpful for setting intentions and making behavior change happen. So now, before you continue with the rest of the book, take a moment to name and commit to the habit(s) you want to work on at this point in your life.

Habit

_____

☐ Does this address the problem at the root level?
☐ Does this fit the shape of your life?

Habit

_____

☐ Does this address the problem at the root level?
☐ Does this fit the shape of your life?

*The most important habit is choosing
the right habit to work on.*

CHECK-IN

*At any moment, you are one good choice away
from a meaningfully better life.*

How are things going so far?

_____

_____

_____

_____

How would you rate your overall progress?

    1   2   3   4   5   6   7   8   9   10

Are your habits continuing to reinforce the identity that you want to build?

_____

_____

_____

_____

What is at least one tiny victory from your work so far?

_____

_____

_____

What's working well? What's not?

_____

_____

_____

What obstacles are holding you back? How can you plan to overcome them?

_____

_____

_____

What have you learned?

_____

_____

_____

People can sometimes be held hostage by their expectations. They have a dream of something they would like to achieve or a path they intend to follow, but their mindset falls apart when things don't work out how they had hoped.

The key is to reach for an extremely high bar but to be adaptable enough to reframe the failures, disappointments, and defeats into fuel for the next thing. Give your best effort, but no matter how it works out, trust that life will be good for you. Focus on how the world is working with you, not against you. Everything you are given is material for the next move. Everything.

PART II

The Four Laws of Behavior Change

Just as atoms are the building blocks of molecules,

atomic habits are the building blocks of remarkable results.

I N "THE SCIENCE of Habit," we discussed the habit loop, the four-step process that occurs every time you perform a habit. These four steps—cue, craving, response, and reward—are the backbone of every habit, and your brain runs through these steps in the same order each time. Together, these four steps form a neurological feedback loop that ultimately allows you to create automatic habits.

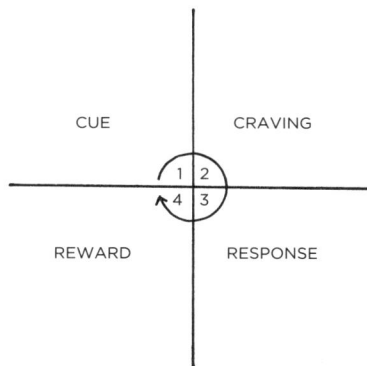

All four steps are necessary to create a habit, which means that if any step in this process doesn't occur, the habit won't form. Eliminate the cue, and the behavior will never be triggered. Reduce the craving, and you won't feel the need to act. Prevent the response and the behavior won't be performed. Make the reward unsatisfying, and even if the behavior has been performed once, you won't want to do it again.

But what does this look like in practice? How do you actually go about eliminating a cue or reducing a craving? The answer is to follow the practical framework of the Four Laws of Behavior Change. The four laws correspond to the four steps of the habit loop, turning them into simple, actionable rules for creating good habits and breaking bad ones. Here they are again, with their corresponding habit-loop step:

The Habit Loop	THE FOUR LAWS OF BEHAVIOR CHANGE	
	Building Good Habits	**Breaking Bad Habits**
1. Cue	The First Law: *Make It Obvious*	The First Law Inverted: *Make It Invisible*
2. Craving	The Second Law: *Make It Attractive*	The Second Law Inverted: *Make It Unattractive*
3. Response	The Third Law: *Make It Easy*	The Third Law Inverted: *Make It Difficult*
4. Reward	The Fourth Law: *Make It Satisfying*	The Fourth Law Inverted: *Make It Unsatisfying*

In the following sections, we will tackle each law, one at a time, looking at strategies for how we can use them to build and break habits.

THE FIRST LAW:
Make It Obvious

THE FIRST LAW of Behavior Change is all about
tackling your habits at the level of the cue—the
thing that triggers your habits. By altering our cues,
we can alter our habits, either to build or break them.
Working with cues is particularly powerful since, as
the first step in the habit loop, they determine whether
a habit even begins. Remove the cue for a bad habit,
and the habit will never start. Create a powerful cue
for a new habit, and you can ensure that you'll actually
start the behavior.

CUE	CRAVING
REWARD	RESPONSE

The First Law of Behavior Change is *make it obvious*. It is the idea that the more
obvious and visible a cue is, the more likely the cue will happen. This is intuitive.
Our habits are cued by triggers in our environment that remind us to perform those
habits, and the easier it is for our brains to perceive those triggers, the more likely it
is that the habit loop will begin.

Of course, the inverse is also true: The more difficult it is for our brains to perceive that trigger, the less likely it is that the habit loop will begin. Make the cue

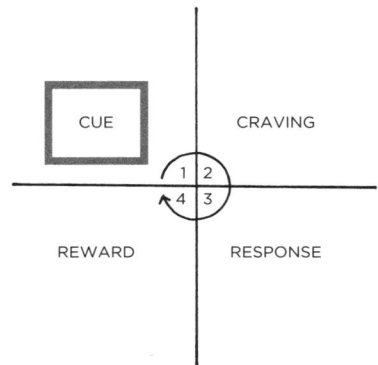

invisible, and the habit will never be triggered in the first place. For this reason, the Inverted First Law of Behavior Change is particularly powerful for breaking habits. If you can cut a bad habit off at the cue, nothing else is needed in order to break it—the habit will simply never be triggered.

Understanding this lever gives us the necessary tools to alter our habits' cues by making them more or less obvious.

In the rest of this section, we will explore practical strategies for using the First Law and its inverse to build and break habits. For the following exercises, you can use the habit(s) that you selected in Part I, or you can select a new habit to focus on.

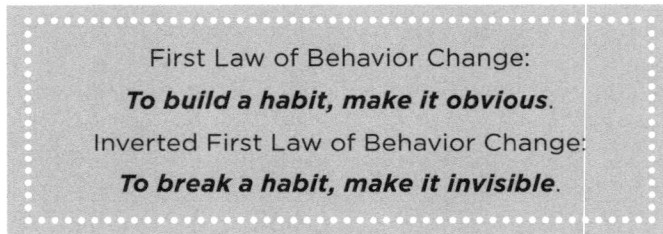

First Law of Behavior Change:
To build a habit, make it obvious.
Inverted First Law of Behavior Change:
To break a habit, make it invisible.

THE FUNDAMENTALS OF CUE CRAFTING

Whether you're aware of it or not, every existing habit has a cue built into it. But if you're trying to adopt a new habit, your new habit will not already have a cue. This may seem obvious, but it's one of the most difficult aspects of building habits. Without a cue to kick off the habit, the habit won't happen, no matter how desperately you want it to.

We've all experienced this in our lives. You want to start calling your family more, and you tell yourself that this is the week your new habit will begin, and yet somehow it never happens. Weeks go by and the calls never happen. The problem is not that you don't want this habit, or that it's too difficult to fit into your life. The problem is that you haven't created a *cue* for your habit, and so there is nothing to trigger it.

When we talk about the First Law—*make it obvious*—the thing that we're trying to make obvious is the habit's cue. The more obvious the cue, the more likely it is that the habit loop will be triggered in our brains, resulting in us completing the action.

So before we look at various ways to make the cue obvious, let's talk about designing the cue itself.

THE FIVE KINDS OF CUES

Most cues fall into five fundamental categories. Understand them, and you can choose which makes the most sense for the habit you're trying to build.

1. **Time**—*Every morning, I make my bed.*
2. **Location**—*Whenever I'm in the kitchen, I check to see if there are dishes to be done.*
3. **Preceding events**—*After I'm done watching TV, I put away the remote.*
4. **Emotional states**—*When I notice that I'm feeling anxious, I pause and take five deep breaths.*
5. **Other people**—*When my friend tells me he's going for a run, I join him.*

The first three are the easiest to work with when designing cues, but any of the five can be a viable option.

Make Better Cues

The key to designing a successful cue is to pick a trigger that is very specific and immediately actionable.

For example, if you want to build a habit of calling long-distance friends more, you might choose a cue like, "After work, I will call a friend who lives in a different city from me." This might work, but the cue is not very specific. When? On Wednesdays, or will you do this every single day? The vagueness makes it harder to know when to do the action and less likely that you will be able to follow through.

But if you choose a cue like "Every Wednesday, as soon as I get in the car to begin my commute home, I will call a friend who lives in a different city from me," then you will know exactly when to perform the behavior, and it is much more likely that you will be able to do so.

The more specific and actionable you make your cue, the better.

IMPLEMENTATION INTENTIONS

Let's look at some evidence-backed strategies for cue creation. There are a number of ways to build cues for your habits and make them obvious, but one of the simplest and most effective is setting *implementation intentions*, a strategy that creates cues based on time and location. Simply put, an implementation intention is the act of taking a habit that you feel *motivated* to do and creating a concrete *plan* for how you will implement it.

Researchers have shown that motivation alone does not have a significant impact on the likelihood that we will perform a given habit. But the simple act of stating a plan does.

The way to apply this strategy to your habits is to fill out this sentence:

I will [BEHAVIOR] at [TIME] in [LOCATION].
   Example: I will WRITE FOR FIVE MINUTES at 8 P.M. in MY LIVING ROOM.

To begin, brainstorm a few time and location pairings when you think it might make sense to cue your new habit.

Habit: _____

    Time: _____ Location: _____

    Time: _____ Location: _____

    Time: _____ Location: _____

Look at what you've brainstormed above and choose one time and location pair to try out. Write your implementation intention below, and then follow it for one week.

Implementation Intention

I will _____ at _____ in _____.

Reflection After One Week: Were you able to follow through with the plan? Why or why not? Do you want to adjust anything about your implementation intention or choose a new time and location pair to try for another week?

_____

_____

_____

_____

    If you want to make changes, do so and then try for another week.

You will see the following line and symbol throughout this workbook. Whenever you do, it means that below it you will find space to complete the exercise an additional time, in case you're working on another habit or are going through the workbook a second time.

↓

Brainstorm a few time and location pairings when you think it might make sense to cue your new habit.

Habit: _____

Time: _____ Location: _____

Time: _____ Location: _____

Time: _____ Location: _____

Look at what you've brainstormed above and choose one time and location pair to try out. Write your implementation intention below, and then follow it for one week.

Implementation Intention

I will _____ at _____ in _____.

Reflection After One Week: Were you able to follow through with the plan? Why or why not? Do you want to adjust anything about your implementation intention or choose a new time and location pair to try for another week?

_____

_____

_____

Implementation intentions can also be a useful tool for breaking habits. Just as having a plan can help you follow through on an intention to perform a habit, it can also help you follow through on an intention to not. To use implementation intentions this way, follow the same implementation intention formula, but instead of creating a new time and location, state your plan to *not* perform your habit at the time and place where you usually do:

I will *not* [BEHAVIOR] at [TIME] in [LOCATION].
Example: I will *not* BITE MY NAILS at NIGHT in BED READING.

Fill out the implementation intention below with the usual time and place where you perform the habit you're trying to break. Set your intention, then try it for a week.

Implementation Intention

I will *not* _____ at _____ in _____ .

Reflection After One Week: Were you able to follow through with the plan? Why or why not? Do you want to adjust anything about your implementation intention or choose a new time and location pair to try for another week?

_____

_____

_____

_____

Fill out the implementation intention below with the usual time and place where you perform the habit you're trying to break. Set your intention, then try it for a week.

Implementation Intention

I will *not* _____ at _____ in _____ .

Reflection After One Week: Were you able to follow through with the plan? Why or why not? Do you want to adjust anything about your implementation intention or choose a new time and location pair to try for another week?

_____

_____

_____

_____

_____

_____

_____

HABIT STACKING

Habit stacking is a specific kind of an implementation intention, but instead of choosing a date and time to tie your new habit to, you stack the new habit on top of a habit that you're already performing reliably.

For instance, if you're trying to start flossing more, you might create a habit stack by tying flossing to the act of brushing your teeth. In this case, you would cue your new habit using the old habit, saying, "Before I brush my teeth, I will floss my teeth."

Here's the habit stacking formula:

Before/After [CURRENT HABIT], I will [NEW HABIT].

The first step of starting a habit stack is to select your trigger habit—the existing habit you're going to link your new habit to.

> **CHOOSING THE RIGHT TRIGGER HABIT**
>
> The key to selecting the right trigger habit is to choose one that has the same cadence and timing as the habit you're trying to create. If you want to go to the gym three days a week, it doesn't make sense to tie this habit to one you perform every day. And if you're trying to read an article first thing every morning, don't tie this habit to one that occurs at the end of your day.

To begin, brainstorm trigger habits you could link your new habit to. Circle whether you will perform your new habit before or after the trigger habit.

Habit: _____

Before/After: _____

Before/After: _____

Before/After: _____

TROUBLE BRAINSTORMING?

Need help brainstorming the right trigger habits? One way to do this is to make a list of the habits that you perform every day without fail, such as brushing your teeth or making a cup of coffee. Choosing this kind of habit as a trigger ensures that the trigger habit will actually happen. Think about which habits you do most reliably and list them below. Then try one out as your trigger habit.

_____   _____
_____   _____
_____   _____
_____   _____

Look at what you've brainstormed, then choose one trigger habit to tie your new habit to and write out your intention to perform this habit stack. Then try the stack for a week.

Habit: _____ Trigger: _____

Before/After_____, I will _____.

Reflection After One Week: Is the habit stack working to cue your new habit? Do you like these habits stacked together? Do you want to choose a new trigger habit to try for another week?

_____

_____

_____

_____

Brainstorm trigger habits you could link your new habit to. Circle whether you will perform your new habit before or after the trigger habit.

Habit: _____

   Before/After: _____

   Before/After: _____

   Before/After: _____

Look at what you've brainstormed, then choose one trigger habit to tie your new habit to and write out your intention to perform this habit stack. Then try the stack for a week.

Habit: _____ Trigger: _____

Before/After_____, I will _____.

Reflection After One Week: Is the habit stack working to cue your new habit? Do you like these habits stacked together? Do you want to choose a new trigger habit to try for another week?

_____

_____

_____

_____

HABIT STACKING IN A ROUTINE

Another way to approach habit stacking is to place a habit in the middle of a routine instead of just tying it to one habit. For this, you can refer to your Habit Scorecards to look at some of the routines you already have in place, or you can use a different routine.

To start, write out your current routine in the left-hand column. Then choose one space to slot your new habit into.

Current Routine   **New Habit**

Now your habit will be cued as part of the routine you already have in place. Try it for a week and then reflect.

Reflection After One Week: Is it working? Do you need to shift where the new habit is in the routine? Do you want to try placing it in a different routine instead? Are there any changes you want to implement before trying it for another week?

_____

_____

_____

_____

PLAN FOR SUCCESS

When and where you choose to insert a habit into your daily routine can make a big difference, so choose your routine wisely. If you try to insert a habit into a routine that already feels rushed and chaotic, it will inevitably be harder to make space for your new habit.

When choosing the routine, ask yourself, "What are the routines during the day when I have the greatest capacity?"

Write out your current routine in the left-hand column. Then choose one space to slot your new habit into.

Current Routine   **New Habit**

Now your habit will be cued as part of the routine you already have in place. Try it for a week and then reflect.

Reflection After One Week: Is it working? Do you need to shift where the new habit is in the routine? Do you want to try placing it in a different routine instead? Are there any changes you want to implement before trying it for another week?

_____

_____

_____

_____

Habit stacking isn't just for building habits. It can also be a great tool for breaking habits. To do this, instead of using an existing habit to cue a new habit, use an existing habit to cue the habit that comes *after* the bad habit, effectively bypassing the bad habit.

For instance, say that every day when you come home from work, the first thing you do is sit down on the couch to watch TV for an hour before eventually moving on to work out and cook dinner. If you want to break the habit of watching TV, create a habit stack where you cut TV out of the routine and instead use walking through the front door to cue changing into your workout clothes. Walking through the front door will now cue working out instead of watching TV. Then the rest of your evening routine can continue as planned, just without the bad habit.

This same habit stacking principle can also be used to replace bad habits in routines. In this scenario, instead of having walking through the door cue the habit *after* watching TV, try having it cue a habit that's an alternative to watching TV, such as reading a book. In this case, you aren't cutting the habit out of the routine; you're swapping it out for a habit that feels more beneficial.

To start, write out your current routine in the left-hand column of the following page. Then, if you're looking to remove a habit, simply circle the habit and use the previous habit to cue the one that comes after. If you're looking to replace the habit, write the replacement habit in the column to the right.

Current Routine   **Replacement Habit**

Try your new stack for a week and then reflect.

Reflection After One Week: Is it working? Have you effectively removed or replaced the bad habit? Do you want to modify your plan and try again for another week?

_____

_____

_____

Write out your current routine in the left-hand column. Then, if you're looking to remove a habit, simply circle the habit and use the previous habit to cue the one that comes after. If you're looking to replace the habit, write the replacement habit in the column to the right.

Current Routine   **Replacement Habit**

Try your new stack for a week and then reflect.

Reflection After One Week: Is it working? Have you effectively removed or replaced the bad habit? Do you want to modify your plan and try again for another week?

_____

_____

_____

_____

The secret to getting results that last is to never stop making improvements.

ADVANCED HABIT STACKING

Are you ready to level up? One of the best things about habit stacking is how scalable it is. Once you have found success with one habit, you can play around with creating bigger stacks of new habits, chaining them together with each habit acting as the cue for the next. The resulting stack will look like this:

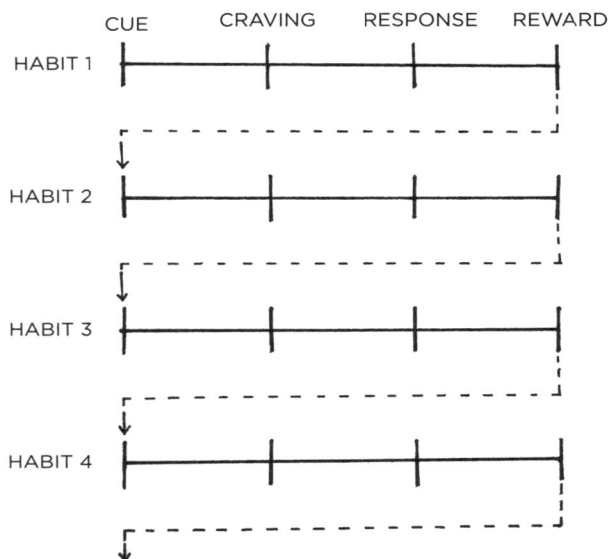

Then take your whole stack and tie it to a single anchor habit or insert it into a current routine. Try it out for yourself to see the power of habit stacking.

MAKING THE AUTOMATIC CONSCIOUS

With a habit that we want to break, the project is a bit different. Instead of creating a new cue, the goal is to eliminate the existing cue—to make it invisible. This is the Inverted First Law of Behavior Change. But before we can eliminate a cue, we need to identify it in the first place, and this can be trickier than you might think.

Habits are, by definition, behaviors that have become automatic. Once a habit is ingrained, it is triggered and performed almost without thought. This automatic nature is part of what makes them so powerful—once a good habit has formed, we need to expend almost no energy to keep doing it. But it also means that most of our habits occur without our conscious awareness, which can make it very difficult to identify and target the cues of the ones we want to break. After all, how can you work to make a cue invisible if you don't know what the cue is?

This is why it's critical to start the habit-breaking process by bringing awareness to the habits we're trying to break. This may seem counterintuitive, since our ultimate goal is to make these cues invisible, but we can't make something invisible until we know what it is in the first place.

To do this, for the habit you are trying to break, write out what you think the habit's cues are, so you can then work to make them invisible. Remember that cues come in all shapes and sizes. Often, cues are visual, but they can be related to other senses as well (for example, if you have a habit of smoking, smelling cigarette smoke might be a cue). Also remember that your habit might have many cues, which is part of why it can be so difficult to break certain habits. The more cues you are able to identify, the more opportunities you will have to cut off your bad habit.

Habit: _____

Cues	

Habit: _____

Cues	

POINTING-AND-CALLING

If you are having trouble identifying your habit's cues, using the simple strategy of *pointing-and-calling* can help. To do this, simply say aloud your habit as you're performing it. As you're reaching for a cigarette, say "I am smoking a cigarette." When you begin scrolling on social media, say "I am scrolling on my phone."

Although it may feel silly to do so, just the act of speaking your habits out loud heightens your awareness of the behaviors you are performing, calling attention to cues that might otherwise be subconscious.

For the next week, take the habit you are trying to break and speak it aloud every time you are performing it. If you are trying to break the habit of biting your nails, say "I am biting my nails" every time you begin to do so, in order to bring awareness to the moment.

Then write down everything you're noticing about the habit and its cue. Essentially, you will be creating a habit stack, with saying your behavior out loud acting as the cue to write down anything you're noticing about the habit you're performing. The goal of this exercise is to help you become conscious of the patterns that your bad habit follows and notice valuable information about its cues.

Habit: _____	
When	
Where	
How Often	
Anything Else You're Noticing	

Habit: _____	
When	
Where	
How Often	
Anything Else You're Noticing	

Pointing-and-calling can also be used to build habits. For the same reasons that it is helpful for bringing awareness to the cues of our bad habits, it can be used to bring awareness to the cues of our good habits—effectively making them more obvious.

If you are trying to leave your phone in another room while you sleep, say "I am leaving my phone outside the bedroom" as you place it on the kitchen counter. If you are trying to drink more water throughout the day, say "I am drinking water" before you take a sip. Just the act of speaking your habits out loud heightens your awareness of the behaviors you are trying to build, making it more likely that you will perform them. In other words, by speaking your habits out loud, you are making them more obvious, calling attention to what might otherwise go unnoticed and forgotten.

Try it for yourself! If you are trying to build a habit, write out the cue you will speak out loud as you are performing the habit.

Habit: _____

Spoken Cue: _____

Try this out for a week and then reflect on your experience.

Reflection After One Week: Was pointing-and-calling effective for you? Are there habits for which you think this strategy might be more or less effective?

_____

_____

_____

_____

_____

_____

Habit: _____

Spoken Cue: _____

Try this out for a week and then reflect on your experience.

Reflection After One Week: Was pointing-and-calling effective for you? Are there habits for which you think this strategy might be more or less effective?

_____

_____

_____

_____

_____

_____

CONTEXT IS EVERYTHING

Now that we've worked on building and identifying cues, let's talk about making them *obvious* or *invisible*. When we talk about making something more or less obvious, what we're really talking about is the degree to which something stands out *in our environment*. Why? Because as much as we'd like to believe that we make decisions independent of our environment, research shows the opposite. The truth is that a large amount of our behavior is motivated not by our conscious motivation and willpower, but by how things are presented to us in our environment, whether we're aware of it or not.

> *Environment is the invisible hand that shapes human behavior.*

Specifically, many of the actions we take each day are shaped not by purposeful drive or choice, but by the most obvious option. We have all experienced this. When you shop in a grocery store, you are more likely to buy whichever brand is at eye level, and if you place a book on your bedside table, you are more likely to pick it up before bed. Lewin's Equation describes this idea in simple terms: *Behavior is a function of the person in their environment.*

We can use this lever to our advantage. The more obvious a cue is, the more likely we are to notice it and have it trigger a habit loop. The less obvious a cue is, the less likely we are to notice it and have it trigger a habit loop. If you want to eat more fruit, you'll be more likely to grab a piece if you keep your fruit in a bowl on the counter instead of in the refrigerator. Want to stop spending so much time playing video games? Store your game console in a closet instead of having it out at all times. Designing our environments to determine how much certain cues stand out is the best way to facilitate behavior change with the First Law.

> *If you want to make a habit a big part of your life, make the cue a big part of your environment.*

Since we perceive our environments with all our senses, cues can take many forms. That being said, vision is the most powerful of all human senses, which means that visual cues are the greatest catalyst for our behavior. And the most persistent behaviors of all usually have *multiple* cues. By sprinkling many triggers throughout your surroundings instead of relying on just one, you increase the odds that you'll think about your habit throughout the day. Even if you miss one cue, you will probably see the next. Making a better decision is easy when the cues for good habits are right in front of you. If a habit you're trying to break has multiple cues, then the task becomes identifying and making invisible as many of them as possible. The fewer cues you are exposed to, the less likely it is that your bad habit will be triggered.

You can see how important it is to live and work in environments that are filled with the cues that prompt your desired habits and that eliminate the cues of the habits you are trying to break. The good news is that you can easily alter the spaces where you live and work to do so. Understanding this principle is the key to learning how to be the architect—instead of the victim—of your environment.

THE MYTH OF SELF-CONTROL

One of the most common beliefs about habits is that the key to sticking with good habits and conquering bad ones is self-control. If we could just increase our discipline, all our problems would be solved. For this reason, we often think that people who are successful must have an above-average amount of willpower.

However, research shows something different: People who appear to have fantastic self-control are actually no better at self-control than anyone else. What they *are* better at is structuring their lives such that they do not *need* more willpower. They set up their lives to avoid temptation.

The key to self-discipline? Structure your environment so that you don't need it! So if you are having trouble avoiding the distraction of social media, instead of expending effort trying to resist your phone, put your phone in another room so that you aren't tempted by it. Take willpower out of the equation.

ENVIRONMENTAL ASSESSMENT

Before you redesign your environment to support your habits, it's important to start by assessing your current situation. Only then will you have the information to determine what needs changing and be able to successfully do so.

To begin, go to a space in your house where you spend a lot of time, and look around. Notice the cues that are obvious—a TV in a central location, a phone charger by the bed, an easily accessible bookshelf. Notice the cues that are hidden—a musical instrument stored in a closet, workout clothes on a high-up shelf, a daily journal stored in a drawer.

Below, write out which habits this space facilitates and which it doesn't, and the cues that make it so.

Space: _____

Habits Facilitated	Obvious Cues	Habits Not Facilitated	Hidden Cues

Now repeat this exercise in the other rooms in your house in which you spend a significant amount of time or in which your relevant habits occur. You can also use this to evaluate a relevant space outside your home, such as your office.

Space: _____

Habits Facilitated	Obvious Cues	Habits Not Facilitated	Hidden Cues

Space: _____

Habits Facilitated	Obvious Cues	Habits Not Facilitated	Hidden Cues

Space: _____

Habits Facilitated	Obvious Cues	Habits Not Facilitated	Hidden Cues

Space: _____

Habits Facilitated	Obvious Cues	Habits Not Facilitated	Hidden Cues

Now take a look at the assessment you've done of your spaces. What are you noticing? What patterns are you seeing in how your spaces are or aren't supporting your habits?

_____

_____

_____

_____

_____

Based on your assessment, which spaces feel the most conducive to your habits and which feel the least?

_____

_____

_____

_____

_____

Do you have any initial ideas about how you want to change those spaces to better support your habits?

_____

_____

_____

_____

_____

_____

DESIGNING YOUR ENVIRONMENT FOR SUCCESS

Now that you've assessed your spaces, let's use the First Law to design your environment for success.

Using your assessment, identify the environment most relevant to the habit you're working on building or breaking. Think carefully about this, as the answer may not be as simple as it seems. For instance, if your goal is to reduce the food waste of produce in your fridge, the relevant environment might be the whole kitchen, or it might be the inside of the refrigerator.

Habit: _____   Environment: _____

Next, draw the space in which this habit occurs. Draw the physical layout of the space, including furniture, as well as the relevant objects within it. Don't worry about being artistic. Rather, the goal is just to get a representation of your habit's environment.

Now take a colored pen and circle the items involved in your target behavior. These items could be big, such as pieces of furniture and their layout, or they could be small, such as light switches and TV remotes. Take a look and assess: What do you notice about the placement of these things? Are they obvious enough? Are they front and center, or are they hidden? Are the items involved in your habit all present, or are some missing? What in your space is creating friction in your routine?

_____

_____

_____

_____

_____

_____

Based on your analysis, brainstorm ways you could redesign your environment to make your cues more or less obvious and facilitate your behavior change. These ideas could be in reaction to your drawing, or they could be new ideas. Do you need to move something so that it's front and center? Do you need to move something out of the room? Think about all the senses, but pay special attention to visual cues. The goal here is to generate as many ideas as possible so that you have many options to try.

Ways to Make It More or Less Obvious:

_____

Habit: _____

_____   _____

_____

_____

Now try implementing as many of these ideas as possible for a week, and then return here to reflect on how it went.

Reflection After One Week: What was the most helpful? Which cues ended up having the greatest impact on the likelihood of you performing the habit? Does anything else need to be changed in your environment to facilitate your behavior change?

_____

_____

_____

_____

_____

_____

First, what is the space that contains the cues for your target habit?

Habit: _____ Environment: _____

Next, draw the space in which this habit occurs. Draw the physical layout of the space, including furniture, as well as the relevant objects within it. Don't worry about being artistic. Rather, the goal is just to get a representation of your habit's environment.

Now take a colored pen and circle the items involved in your target behavior. These items could be big, such as pieces of furniture and their layout, or they could be small, such as light switches and TV remotes. Take a look and assess: What do you notice about the placement of these things? Are they obvious enough? Are they front and center, or are they hidden? Are the items involved in your habit all present, or are some missing? What in your space is creating friction in your routine?

_____

_____

_____

_____

_____

Based on your analysis, brainstorm ways you could redesign your environment to make your cues more or less obvious and facilitate your behavior change. These ideas could be in reaction to your drawing, or they could be new ideas. Do you need to move something so that it's front and center? Do you need to move something out of the room? Think about all the senses, but pay special attention to visual cues. The goal here is to generate as many ideas as possible so that you have many options to try.

Ways to Make It More or Less Obvious:

_____

Habit:

_____

_____

_____

_____

_____

Now try implementing as many of these ideas as possible for a week and then return here to reflect on how it went.

Reflection After One Week: What was the most helpful? Which cues ended up having the greatest impact on the likelihood of you performing the habit? Does anything else need to be changed in your environment to facilitate your behavior change?

_____

_____

_____

_____

_____

ADVANCED ENVIRONMENTAL DESIGN

Sometimes creating a space that's conducive to your habits requires more than just making small changes to your current space. The reason for this is that over time, through repeated use and experience, an environment will become deeply associated with the behaviors you do in it, making it difficult to change your associations with the space. If your living room is where you always relax and watch TV, it will be difficult to rewire your brain to associate it with productivity and work. If you associate your bed with watching TV and reading, you might find that it's difficult to fall asleep in bed. Put another way, while an environment may contain individual cues for your habits, over time, the entire environment becomes a cue for your habits.

What this means is that it can be easier to change your habits—or start new ones—in a new environment that does not contain old associations or memories. If you're newly working from home and struggling to be productive in your kitchen, you might have more luck working in your living room or spare bedroom. If you're trying to start an exercise routine but associate your living room with relaxing, you might have more luck working out in the park.

That being said, it's not always easy or feasible to find a new space for your new habit. In that case, try creating a "new" space within a current space. For instance, if you're trying to create a writing habit and are struggling to do so in your current space, try moving a chair and lamp into a corner of the current room in order to create a writing nook for yourself. Even though this is not a totally new space, just the act of rearranging some furniture can have the same effect.

ONE SPACE, ONE USE

Whenever possible, avoid mixing the context of one habit with another. If a space is meant to cue multiple habits, the easier one will always win out, making it harder to perform the other one. For instance, if you're trying to have your living room cue both doing work and watching TV, watching TV will always win out.

    To prevent this, I always try to follow this principle: One space, one use.

For the habit you're working on, think about whether creating an entirely new space would be helpful, either by seeking one out or by redesigning a current space so that it *feels* new.

Habit: _____

Would performing this habit in a new or different environment help facilitate it? How so?

_____

_____

_____

_____

_____

_____

_____

_____

If you think it would, brainstorm some ways that you could create this new space. Could you find a new space entirely? If so, what would it look like? If creating an entirely new space is not an option or feels unnecessary, how could you redesign your current space to adhere to the principle of "one space, one use"?

_____

_____

_____

_____

_____

_____

Habit: _____

Would performing this habit in a new or different environment help facilitate it? How so?

_____

_____

_____

_____

_____

If you think it would, brainstorm some ways that you could create this new space. Could you find a new space entirely? If so, what would it look like? If creating an entirely new space is not an option or feels unnecessary, how could you redesign your current space to adhere to the principle of "one space, one use"?

_____

_____

_____

_____

_____

The people with the best self-control are typically the ones who need to use it the least. Perseverance, grit, and willpower are essential to success, and the way to improve these qualities is not by wishing you were a more disciplined person, but by creating a more disciplined environment.

Reflect on this quote. How does it apply to your life and habits, and what can you learn from it?

_____

_____

_____

_____

_____

_____

_____

_____

_____

CONCLUSION: THE FIRST LAW OF BEHAVIOR CHANGE

Now it's your turn. Based on what you've learned through these exercises, list out how you're going to use the First Law of Behavior Change to influence the obviousness of your habits. Think about what's worked for you and what hasn't, and feel free to combine principles in new ways. The goal is not to follow a template, but rather to experiment and find what works for *you*.

Habit: _____

How Will You Use the First Law to Support Your Behavior Change?

Habit: _____

How Will You Use the First Law to Support Your Behavior Change?

Look at what you've written and make a commitment to implement these strategies. These will act as the foundation for your habits as we move forward with the remaining three laws of behavior change.

CHEAT SHEET: THE FIRST LAW OF BEHAVIOR CHANGE

*The First Law of Behavior Change is **Make It Obvious.***
To build a habit, make it obvious.

Key Principles	Exercises
Craft Strong, Obvious Cues ■ Build cues to trigger new habits. The more obvious the cue, the more likely it is to trigger the habit ■ Use the five cue types: time, location, preceding events, emotional states, other people ■ Pick cues that are specific and immediately actionable	■ Use implementation intentions: "I will [BEHAVIOR] at [TIME] in [LOCATION]" ■ Use habit stacking: "Before/After I [CURRENT HABIT], I will [NEW HABIT]" ○ Use single stacks, routine stacks, and larger stacks ■ Pointing-and-calling makes habits obvious

Design Your Environment
■ Behavior is a function of your environment
■ Design your environment to make your cues as obvious as possible
  ○ Cues can use any of your senses, but visual cues are the strongest
  ○ Sprinkle your environment with multiple cues
■ It can be easier to start a new habit in a new space
■ One space, one use
	■ Redesign your environment to make the cues of good habits obvious and visible
	■ Choose a new space to perform your new habit in
	■ Section off a space within your current environment

*The Inverted First Law of Behavior Change is **Make It Invisible.***
To break a habit, make it invisible.

Key Principles	Exercises
Identify Your Cues and Make Them Invisible	■ Use pointing-and-calling to identify cues
Rewire the Cues of Bad Habits	■ Use habit stacking to rewire current cues
Design Your Environment ■ Behavior is a function of your environment ■ Design your environment to make your cues as invisible as possible	■ Redesign your environment to make the cues of bad habits invisible
Self-Control Is a Myth ■ The secret to self-control is to not have to use it ■ People who seem to have better self-control really just spend their time in less tempting situations	■ Instead of spending energy avoiding the temptation of bad habits, design your environment to reduce temptation as much as possible

CHECK-IN

Treat failure like a scientist. Each attempt is an experiment.
Each mistake is a clue. You're not failing. You're refining.

How are things going so far?

_____

_____

How would you rate your overall progress?

      1   2   3   4   5   6   7   8   9   10

Are your habits continuing to reinforce the identity that you want to build?

_____

_____

_____

_____

What is at least one tiny victory from your work so far?

_____

_____

_____

What's working well? What's not?

_____

_____

_____

_____

What obstacles are holding you back? How can you plan to overcome them?

_____

_____

_____

What have you learned?

_____

_____

_____

_____

What single habit, if implemented consistently for

the rest of this year, would transform your life the most?

THE SECOND LAW:
Make It Attractive

THE SECOND LAW of Behavior Change—*make it attractive*—looks at how we can influence our habits at the level of the craving, or the thing that makes us *want* to perform them. When we are about to perform a habit, the craving kicks in, telling us that the result will be desirable. It is the *prediction* of a good reward. And notably, it is this anticipation of a reward—not the fulfillment of the reward—that gets us to take action. We order french fries because we *anticipate* that they will taste delicious, we open social media apps because we *anticipate* that scrolling will make us feel entertained, and we pour ourselves a drink because we *anticipate* that it will make us feel relaxed and happy.

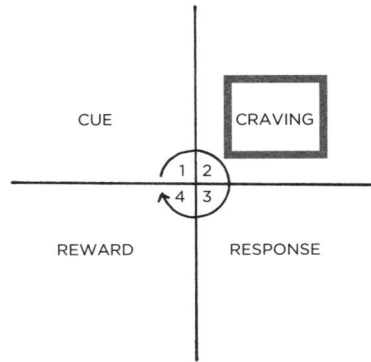

THE DOPAMINE FEEDBACK LOOP

Most of us are familiar with the dopamine-driven feedback loop, the idea that when you experience pleasure, your brain releases dopamine, which makes you motivated to experience it again.

However, research shows that after that first pleasurable experience, your brain actually begins releasing dopamine *twice*: once when you experience pleasure and once when you *anticipate* it. This is why cravings are so powerful—because *anticipation* of a reward is just as powerful, or even more so, than receiving the reward itself.

This is the power of the Second Law in action—we do the things we crave. The more attractive and enticing you make a behavior, the more likely it is that you'll want to do it. In other words, if you want to do something, you will. So if you want to make yourself do something, you have to figure out how to make yourself *want* to do it.

If we do the things we crave, then the inverse is intuitive: It's much more difficult to work up the desire to do the things that we don't crave. This is why the inverse of the Second Law of Behavior Change is *make it unattractive*. If you want to stop doing a behavior, *decrease* the craving by making the behavior unattractive, and you are much less likely to do it.

In the rest of this section, we will explore practical strategies to use the Second Law and its inverse to build and break habits. For the following exercises, you can use the habit(s) that you selected in Part I, or you can select new habits to focus on.

The Second Law of Behavior Change:

To build a habit, make it attractive.

The Inverted Second Law of Behavior Change:

To break a habit, make it unattractive.

What's the one action that moves the needle more than one hundred other actions? What's the one choice that renders one thousand other choices irrelevant?

TEMPTATION BUNDLING

To build new habits, we need to figure out how to make them attractive so that we naturally begin to crave them. The difficulty with this is that often the habits that we're trying to build aren't attractive on their own. As much as we might want the effects of starting an exercise routine or being quicker to respond to emails, these habits are not intrinsically attractive on their own.

Temptation bundling solves this problem by bundling together your new habit with one that you already find attractive. Link the two, and you'll begin to crave the new habit by association. For instance, if you are trying to do more push-ups but you *want* to watch TV, do ten push-ups every time you watch an episode, and you'll find that you're excited to do the push-ups because it means you get to watch TV.

Another result of bundling the habit you *need* with the habit you *want* is that over time, you'll develop lasting positive associations with the new habit. Which means that after a while, even if you unbundle the habits, you'll still feel positively about the new habit. If you've bundled together TV and push-ups for long enough, you'll still crave the push-ups, even without the TV.

To practice temptation bundling, start by identifying some habits that you already perform that you find very attractive.

_____   _____

_____   _____

_____   _____

Next, look at the habit you're trying to build and choose one of the attractive habits you brainstormed to bundle it with.

New Habit: _____

Attractive Habit: _____

Plan how you will bundle them together:

_____

_____

_____

Try to bundle the habits together for a week, and then come back to reflect.

Reflection After One Week: Is the temptation bundle making your new habit more attractive? Do you like these habits bundled together? Do you want to choose a new attractive habit and try bundling them together for another week?

_____

_____

_____

_____

Identify some habits that you already perform that you find very attractive.

_____   _____

_____   _____

_____   _____

Look at the habit you're trying to build and choose one of the attractive habits you brainstormed to bundle it with.

New Habit: _____

Attractive Habit: _____

Plan how you will bundle them together:

_____

_____

_____

Try to bundle the habits together for a week, and then come back to reflect.

Reflection After One Week: Is the temptation bundle making your new habit more attractive? Do you like these habits bundled together? Do you want to choose a new attractive habit and try bundling them together for another week?

_____

_____

_____

_____

Another way to practice temptation bundling is to combine it with habit stacking, which creates a set of rules to guide your behavior. To do this, choose a habit that you're already performing, and then use it to kick off your new/attractive habit pair. Here is the formula:

1. After I [CURRENT HABIT], I will [NEW HABIT].
2. After [HABIT I NEED], I will [ATTRACTIVE HABIT].

Use your current habits, the habit you're trying to build, and the habits you find attractive to brainstorm possible habit stacks:

After I _____, I will _____, then I will _____.

After I _____, I will _____, then I will _____.

After I _____, I will _____, then I will _____.

After I _____, I will _____, then I will _____.

Practice one of these options for bundling the habits together for a week and then reflect on how it's going.

Reflection After One Week: Do you like this pairing? Are you more motivated to perform the new habit? Do you need to choose a new attractive habit to bundle with the less attractive one?

_____

_____

_____

_____

_____

Use your current habits, the habit you're trying to build, and the habits you find attractive to brainstorm possible habit stacks:

After I _____, I will _____, then I will _____.

After I _____, I will _____, then I will _____.

After I _____, I will _____, then I will _____.

After I _____, I will _____, then I will _____.

Practice one of these options for bundling the habits together for a week and then reflect on how it's going.

Reflection After One Week: Do you like this pairing? Are you more motivated to perform the new habit? Do you need to choose a new attractive habit to bundle with the less attractive one?

_____

_____

_____

_____

_____

_____

MOTIVATION RITUALS

When we talk about the attractiveness of our habits, what we're really talking about are the feelings we associate with them. Habits are attractive when we associate them with positive feelings, and they're unattractive when we associate them with negative ones.

Temptation bundling is one way to make sure your new habit is linked to positive feelings. Another way is to create a motivation ritual. A motivation ritual is an activity that you associate with positive feelings. Because of this pairing, performing it before a new habit will transfer those positive feelings to the new habit, making it feel more attractive. There are two phases to this.

Phase 1

1. Identify the feeling you would like to be able to associate with your new habit, such as happiness, motivation, or excitement: _____

2. Choose an activity that already makes you feel the desired emotion deeply. For instance, petting your dog or practicing a sport. Brainstorm a few here and then choose one:

_____   _____

_____   _____

3. Create a short, simple ritual that you can perform before you do the chosen activity. For instance, taking two deep breaths and smiling, or rolling your shoulders and jumping in place a few times. Or maybe it's doing a visualization. Short mantras can also work really well for this. Write your ritual below (it can be fewer than four steps).

Step 1: _____

Step 2: _____

Step 3: _____

Step 4: _____

4. Practice performing your ritual with your positive activity until the two feel completely intertwined and give you a positive feeling. Now you have a ritual that is encoded with the feelings of the positive activity.

Phase 2

The next step is to apply this ritual to the habit. For example, are you giving a tough presentation but want to feel calm? Do the new ritual that you associate with calm feelings before presenting.

Try building a ritual and applying it to a habit you want to build. Note that this strategy takes time, but once a ritual is encoded with a feeling, it can be hugely helpful.

Reflect on the process below:

_____

_____

_____

_____

_____

Phase 1

1. Identify the feeling you would like to be able to associate with your new habit, such as happiness, motivation, or excitement: _____

2. Choose an activity that already makes you feel the desired emotion deeply. For instance, petting your dog or practicing a sport. Brainstorm a few here and then choose one:

_____   _____

_____   _____

3. Create a short, simple ritual that you can perform before you do the chosen activity. For instance, taking two deep breaths and smiling, or rolling your shoulders and jumping in place a few times. Or maybe it's doing a visualization. Short mantras can also work really well for this. Write your ritual below (it can be fewer than four steps).

Step 1: _____

Step 2: _____

Step 3: _____

Step 4: _____

4. Practice performing your ritual with your positive activity until the two feel completely intertwined and give you a positive feeling. Now you have a ritual that is encoded with the feelings of the positive activity.

Phase 2

The next step is to apply this ritual to the habit. For example, are you giving a tough presentation but want to feel calm? Do the new ritual that you associate with calm feelings before presenting.

   Try building a ritual and applying it to a habit you want to build. Note that this strategy takes time, but once a ritual is encoded with a feeling, it can be hugely helpful.

Reflect on the process below:

_____

_____

_____

_____

_____

MAKING IT FUN

Another way you can make your habits more attractive is to make them fun. We often think that in order for a habit to be good for us, it needs to be a chore. We expect that while our good habits will pay off in the future, they will be a drag in the present.

The problem with this is that expecting our good habits to be unenjoyable is the opposite of craving them, and so is an active barrier to adopting them. And while we can work around this by bundling a less-than-fun habit with an enjoyable one, or by creating a motivation ritual, another solution is to reconceive your habit in its most fun version. Nine times out of ten, the fun version of your habit will be just as good for you as the not-fun version, and the fact that it's way more likely to stick means that, ultimately, the fun version will be much more beneficial.

I remember my friend Tim Ferriss once telling me that when he was working on building a meditation practice, he made it fun by listening to Prince's music. For him, this simple shift turned what had been a chore into something he genuinely enjoyed and looked forward to.

Every habit has a fun version; you just have to find it. If you want to exercise more but find running or weight lifting boring, try a dance class or going for a hike with friends. If you want to read more but find nonfiction dull, try reading thrillers or romances.

On the next page, for the habit that you're working on, ask yourself, "What would it look like if it was fun?" Or "What is the fun version of this habit?" And then brainstorm ways you can make that happen.

Habit: _____

What would it look like if it was fun, and how could you make it so?

_____

_____

_____

_____

_____

Try out this fun version of your habit for a week, and then come back to reflect.

Reflection After One Week: Did making your habit fun make it more attractive? Were you more likely to perform it? Do you want to make any changes and try again?

_____

_____

_____

_____

_____

For the habit that you're working on, ask yourself, "What would it look like if it was fun?" Or "What is the fun version of this habit?" And then brainstorm ways you can make that happen.

Habit: _____

What would it look like if it was fun, and how could you make it so?

_____

_____

_____

_____

Try out this fun version of your habit for a week, and then come back to reflect.

Reflection After One Week: Did making your habit fun make it more attractive? Were you more likely to perform it? Do you want to make any changes and try again?

_____

_____

_____

_____

IDENTIFYING YOUR CRAVINGS

Ask yourself this question three times and try to refine and improve your answer each time: What do I really want?

When we're trying to break a habit, the task looks a little different. Instead of trying to *induce* a craving, the goal is to *eliminate* the craving so that you *don't want* to perform the habit you're trying to break. This is the Inverted Second Law of Behavior Change—*make it unattractive.*

But to eliminate a craving, we must first identify it. Only then can we accurately target it and work to make it unattractive.

IDENTIFYING THE MOMENT OF CRAVING

Locating the moment of craving can be difficult. For a deeply entrenched habit, the craving will be so automatic, and the shift from wanting to doing the behavior so fast, it can be tough to find that moment and pause. So don't worry if this is proving hard—just keep trying.

One thing that can help is remembering that the craving is instantly triggered by the cue, which means that you can do this craving-finding process in tandem with the cue-finding process we discussed previously.

Use techniques like pointing-and-calling to notice the cue, and immediately after doing so, note the craving you're experiencing. Essentially, create a habit stack for identifying the cue and identifying the craving.

On the next page, for the habit that you're trying to break, try to pause when you find yourself *wanting* to do the habit. This usually occurs right before you perform the behavior. Pause and write down everything you notice about how you're feeling in this moment: thoughts, feelings, bodily sensations. Don't try to fix anything at this stage—the goal is just to observe.

Habit: _____

Moment of Craving: _____

_____

_____

_____

_____

_____

⟳ ···

Habit: _____

Moment of Craving: _____

_____

_____

_____

_____

Now look at what you noticed for your habit and think: What were you *craving* in that moment? In other words, why did you want to perform the habit? There are usually two layers to this: a surface-level craving and a deeper craving. Let's identify them both.

THE LAYERS OF CRAVINGS

Although the top layer of your craving may feel very straightforward—"I was craving a cigarette because I wanted a cigarette"—the *real* craving is the deeper feeling underneath, perhaps the desire to feel less stressed or to reduce physical discomfort. Whenever we crave something, what we are really experiencing is the desire to change our internal state—to *feel* different. And when we perform a habit, we are *predicting* that the habit will achieve the change we desire. So to find this deeper layer, ask yourself: What do you think will *change* once you perform the habit? The answer is usually a feeling—"I think I will feel calmer, more connected, more accepted." Identifying the deeper craving not only gives us the tools to eliminate it but also helps us understand what we are really craving so that we can fulfill this need in a better, more positive way.

Habit	Surface-Level Craving	Deeper Craving

Habit	Surface-Level Craving	Deeper Craving

THE POWER OF A MINDSET SHIFT

One way to make the habits you're trying to break less attractive is through a simple mindset shift. As we discussed, we crave habits because we expect them to bring us benefits. But if you can employ a mindset shift to convince yourself that, in fact, the habit will *not* bring you these benefits, then you will have no reason to perform the habit in the first place.

To do this, take the habit you are trying to break and look at what you identified as your reasons for craving it. Next, write out the reasons why the habit is *not* actually effective at fulfilling this craving. Then write out what the *benefits* would be to you if you didn't perform the habit. What would be positive about not performing the habit? The goal is to decrease the attractiveness of performing the habit and to increase the attractiveness of not.

Habit: _____

Craving	Why It's Ineffective at Fulfilling the Craving	Benefits of *Not* Doing the Habit

Habit: _____

Craving	Why It's Ineffective at Fulfilling the Craving	Benefits of *Not* Doing the Habit

Mindset shifts aren't only for breaking habits—they can be a powerful tool for building them as well. Just as a mindset shift can make bad habits seem unattractive, it can also make good habits—especially hard ones—seem more attractive by associating them with positive feelings.

The trick is to shift how we talk about our hard habits to emphasize the positives instead of the negatives. Instead of "I *have to* get up to go for a run," it's "I *get* to take the time to care for my body." Instead of "I need to save money this month," it's "I'm building my financial freedom and stability." Try it out on the next page.

Habit: _____

Negative Mindset	Positive Mindset

Habit: _____

Negative Mindset	Positive Mindset

CHOOSING A NEW SOLUTION

Every time you perform a habit, your mind is trying to solve a problem through that internal-state change we discussed earlier. If the craving is the *problem*, then the habit is the *solution*. Perform the habit, and the problem will be addressed, though maybe not in a way you'd prefer. But just because a habit is bad doesn't mean that the craving is bad or should be ignored. Wanting to feel loved or calm or connected is a natural feeling that needs to be addressed, which means that simply trying to ignore the craving is ineffective and will likely lead to you performing your chosen solution—the bad habit—again.

Instead, swap out the bad habit for a better habit that still answers the craving. Scrolling on social media because you're stressed? When you feel the urge, try squeezing a stress ball or doing a five-minute meditation instead. Drinking too much coffee because you want to break up the workday? Still take these breaks, but try swapping out coffee for water, tea, or a flavored seltzer.

Below, for the habit that you're trying to break, write out the cravings and then write out a better way that you could address the craving in the moment.

Craving (the Problem)	Current Habit	Alternative Habit (New Solution)

Next time you feel the craving, try performing your alternative habit instead. Attempt this for a week and then reflect on how it's going.

Reflection After One Week: Did the new habit address the craving? What worked, and what was difficult? Do you need to change how you're identifying the craving or try a different alternative habit?

_____

_____

_____

_____

_____

_____

_____

_____

For the habit that you're trying to break, write out the cravings and then write out a better way that you could address the craving in the moment.

Craving (the Problem)	Current Habit	Alternative Habit (New Solution)

Next time you feel the craving, try performing your alternative habit instead. Attempt this for a week and then reflect on how it's going.

Reflection After One Week: Did the new habit address the craving? What worked, and what was difficult? Do you need to change how you're identifying the craving or try a different alternative habit?

_____

_____

_____

_____

THE POWER OF SOCIAL INFLUENCE

The culture we live in determines which behaviors are attractive to us.

Just as the physical environment is a major factor when it comes to using the First Law, the social environment is a major factor when it comes to using the Second Law. This is because social desirability is the biggest factor in determining the attractiveness of our habits.

Humans are social creatures by design. It is hard to overstate the degree to which we want to fit in, feel like we belong, and earn the approval and respect of our peers. This means that our social environment—the people and groups we seek approval from—hugely influences our habits. We are much more likely to do the behaviors that are valued and normalized by the groups we belong to and the people we're close to. If you're part of a friend group that often meets at a bar, you may find yourself drinking alcohol frequently. If you're part of a running club, you will probably end up spending a lot of time running. You will do these habits not necessarily because you independently value them, but because the group values them.

This is an especially important concept to understand in the age of social media, where social pressure is more intense than ever. We are influenced both by what we see others doing and by the feedback that we get on our content, and understanding the effect that this has on our behavior and choices is crucial.

This means that our social environment is one of the biggest ways that we can influence our habits. If you're a part of a group where a certain habit is the normal behavior, performing this habit will be easy for you. But if you're a part of a group where a certain behavior is not the norm, performing it will be difficult. And trying to change your behavior away from the norms of a group is very challenging.

You can use this lever to your advantage when building and breaking habits by joining the groups that practice the habits you want and leaving the groups that perform habits you don't want. Align your social environment to your habits, and you'll be well on your path to success.

SOCIAL ENVIRONMENT ASSESSMENT

Before you can begin designing a social environment that supports your habits, it's important to assess your current social landscape. Only then will you have the information to determine what needs changing. Remember that these questions are just about noticing, not passing judgment, and that you will surface things that feel both positive and negative.

What groups are you a part of, what habits do they encourage/value/normalize, and what does that encouragement or normalization look like? As you identify your groups, remember the few, the many, and the powerful. And remember that groups can come in all forms: formal activity groups, friend groups, family, colleagues, and communities of identity, just to name a few.

Groups	Habits They Value/ Normalize	How Do They Show This?

WHO ARE THE INFLUENCERS?

We imitate the habits of three groups in particular. Consider each as you're designing your social environment for success.

The Close—We imitate those around us, often subconsciously.

The Many—We follow the consensus of the group, even when we think it's wrong.

The Powerful—We copy those we see as powerful because we desire that power ourselves.

How are the communities that you're a part of influencing your habits?

_____

_____

_____

_____

_____

How have you seen your habits change since being a part of these communities?

_____

_____

_____

_____

_____

_____

How are the groups that you're a part of influencing your goals and the things that you value?

_____

_____

_____

_____

_____

Which groups make you feel the best?

_____

_____

_____

_____

_____

_____

Which make you feel most like who you want to be?

_____

_____

_____

_____

_____

Do any groups that you're in feel detrimental to the habits that you're trying to build?

_____

_____

_____

_____

When changing your habits means challenging the tribe,

change is unattractive. When change means fitting in,

change is very attractive.

SUPPORTING YOUR HABITS SOCIALLY

Now let's look at how you can design a social environment that supports the habits you want to build but not the ones you want to break.

Use your assessment answers to really think about the groups you belong to. Do they truly support your desired behavior change through their norms and values? Do any not? Then think if there are other groups that you are not yet a part of that could better encourage the behavior change.

Habit: _____

Current Groups That Support Your Behavior Change	
Current Groups That Don't Support Your Behavior Change	
Other Groups That Could Encourage This	

Based on what you wrote, do you want to join any groups to support your behavior change? If so, write out a plan for how you would do this, such as researching running groups near you.

_____

_____

_____

_____

_____

Do you want to rethink your exposure to any groups to support your behavior change? If so, write out a plan for how you would do this.

_____

_____

_____

_____

_____

Habit: _____

Current Groups That Support Your Behavior Change	
Current Groups That Don't Support Your Behavior Change	
Other Groups That Could Encourage This	

Based on what you wrote, do you want to join any groups to support your behavior change? If so, write out a plan for how you would do this, such as researching running groups near you.

_____

_____

_____

_____

_____

_____

Do you want to rethink your exposure to any groups to support your behavior change? If so, write out a plan for how you would do this.

_____

_____

_____

_____

_____

_____

FINDING THE RIGHT SUPPORT PARTNERS

When you choose your friends today, you are choosing your habits tomorrow.

The principles of support don't just apply to the groups we join. They apply to our individual relationships as well: romantic, platonic, familial, professional. Identifying which relationships support the behavior change we're looking for—and which don't—is vital to making your habits attractive.

What are the three to five relationships that most significantly impact your daily life?

_____

_____

_____

_____

_____

_____

_____

_____

Which relationships in your life drain you? Which make you feel energized?

_____

_____

_____

_____

_____

With which people do you feel most like who you want to be?

_____

_____

_____

_____

_____

Which relationships best support the behavior change you're trying to make in your life? How can you use this to help yourself?

_____

_____

_____

_____

_____

Do any relationships in your life feel detrimental to your habits? If so, how do you want to navigate that?

_____

_____

_____

_____

_____

_____

Based on what you wrote, for the habit that you're working on, identify the people who will best support you on your behavior-change journey and what you'd like that support to look like.

Habit: _____

Who Will Support You?	
How Will They Support You?	

Habit: _____

Who Will Support You?	
How Will They Support You?	

CONCLUSION: THE SECOND LAW OF BEHAVIOR CHANGE

Now it's your turn. Based on what you've learned through these exercises, list out how you're going to use the Second Law of Behavior Change to influence the attractiveness of your habits. Think about what's worked for you and what hasn't, and feel free to combine principles in new ways. The goal is not to follow a template, but rather to experiment and find what works for *you*.

Habit: _____

How Will You Use the Second Law to Support Your Behavior Change?

Habit: _____

How Will You Use the Second Law to Support Your Behavior Change?

Look at what you've written and make a commitment to implement these strategies. These will act as the foundation for your habits as we move forward with the remaining two laws of behavior change.

CHEAT SHEET: THE SECOND LAW OF BEHAVIOR CHANGE

*The Second Law of Behavior Change is **Make It Attractive.***
To build a habit, make it attractive.

Key Principles	Exercises
Create Cravings ■ Habits are attractive when we associate them with positive feelings ■ New habits are not yet associated with positive feelings, so we need to *make* them something we crave	■ Use temptation bundling. Pair an action you *need* to do with an action you *want* to do. ■ Make your habits fun ■ Create a motivation ritual ■ Reframe your mindset. Highlight the benefits of performing your good habits.
Social Environment Design ■ Our social environment—groups we're a part of and relationships we're in—is the biggest determiner of the attractiveness of our habits	■ Design your social environment to support your changing habits ■ Join a culture where your desired behavior is the normal behavior

*The Inverted Second Law of Behavior Change is **Make It Unattractive.***
To break a habit, make it unattractive.

Key Principles	Exercises
Identify Cravings ■ Identify why you crave your bad habits so that you can address these cravings ■ Habits are solutions to your cravings. If you identify your craving, you can find a better solution for it.	■ Use pointing-and-calling to notice your cravings as they occur ■ Find alternative habits to fit your cravings
Make Your Bad Habits Unattractive	■ Reframe your mindset. Highlight the benefits of avoiding your bad habits.
Social Environment Design ■ Our social environment—groups we're a part of and relationships we're in—is the biggest determiner of the attractiveness of our habits	■ Design your social environment to support your changing habits ■ Leave the groups that enable your bad habits, and join groups that support changing them

CHECK-IN

Savor the little victories as much as you criticize the little mistakes.

How are things going so far?

_____

_____

_____

_____

How would you rate your overall progress?

1   2   3   4   5   6   7   8   9   10

Are your habits continuing to reinforce the identity that you want to build?

_____

_____

_____

_____

_____

What is at least one tiny victory from your work so far?

_____

_____

_____

What's working well? What's not?

_____

_____

_____

What obstacles are holding you back? How can you plan to overcome them?

_____

_____

_____

What have you learned?

_____

_____

_____

Can my current habits carry me

to my desired future?

THE THIRD LAW:
Make It Easy

THE THIRD LAW of Behavior Change—*make it easy*—is about influencing your habits at the level of the response, or the moment when the habit is actually performed. When we think about what makes us perform certain behaviors, we tend to think that our behavior is determined by motivation. If we're having trouble performing a habit, we chastise ourselves, believing that a lack of motivation is to blame. But this doesn't take into account the reality of human psychology.

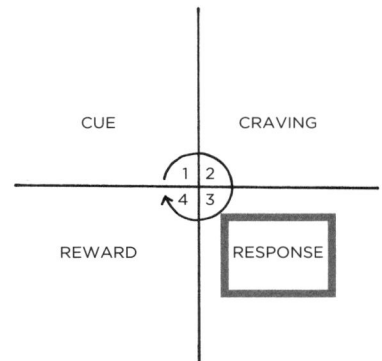

Evolutionarily, we are programmed to follow the Law of Least Effort, which states that when deciding between two similar options, people will naturally gravitate toward the option that delivers the most value for the least amount of work, or energy. In other words, we are predisposed to do what is easy. Which means that when it comes to our habits, the great determiner of whether we perform them is not motivation, but friction, or how easy they are to perform. While a great deal of motivation can help you power through even the most difficult of behaviors, motivation requires a lot of energy and is inevitably variable. Relying on motivation alone to make your habits happen is a surefire way to end up not performing them. But if you make your habits *easy*, you ensure that they can be performed even when motivation is low.

> ••
>
> ### THE HABIT LINE
>
> Behaviors become habits when they become automatic. This threshold is known as the *Habit Line*, and it is reached not by performing a habit for a certain *amount* of time, but by performing it a certain *number* of times. Habits are formed through frequent repetition. In other words, if you want to form a habit, you need to practice it.
>
> This is the other reason why the Third Law is important: because building a habit requires that you repeat it many, many times. And the best way to ensure that you do that is to make each repetition as easy as possible.
>
> ••

This is the Third Law of Behavior Change, and it is simple but powerful. To build a habit, *make it easy to perform.* The inverse is also true: to break a habit, *make it difficult.* In other words, the key to doing desired behaviors is to make them as easy as possible. And the key to stopping unwanted behaviors is to make them as difficult as possible to perform.

In the rest of this section, we will explore practical strategies to use the Third Law and its inverse to build and break habits. For the following exercises, you can use the habit(s) that you selected in Part I, or you can select new habits to focus on.

> The Third Law of Behavior Change:
> **To build a habit, make it easy.**
> The Inverted Third Law of Behavior Change:
> **To break a habit, make it difficult.**

THE TWO-MINUTE RULE

When we try to change our behavior, one of the most common mistakes is trying to do too much in the beginning. It's easy to get excited and jump right into training for a marathon, meditating for an hour every day, or reading a book every week. But while these habits may be positive, they are difficult to maintain in the long term, especially when you're starting from zero. If you go from not running at all to training for a 10K, you are likely to burn out and abandon the habit.

When you're planning a behavior change, it's crucial to start with the easiest version of the habit—the version you can actually stick with—and then scale it up from there. This can be difficult to accept if you're excited about making radical change in your life. But it won't matter how perfect your habit is if it's too difficult to actually get off the ground. Instead, remember that an imperfect start can always be improved upon. The version of your habit that you *can* stick with will help you more than the version that you *can't*. Start now. Optimize later.

> *Instead of planning for what you can complete only on your best day, optimize for what you can stick to even on your worst days.*

REINFORCING IDENTITY-BASED HABITS

The two-minute version of your habits is also helpful because even though it's small, it casts a vote for the identity you're trying to build, helping kick-start the identity-habit feedback loop that is crucial in driving behavior change.

Even if you know you should be starting small, it can be easy to bite off more than you can chew. The best way to counteract this tendency is to use the *Two-Minute Rule*, which states, "When you start a new habit, it should take less than two minutes to do." In other words, *a new habit should not feel like a challenge*. The idea here is that the two-minute version of your habit has a very high likelihood of being repeated. Once you've started doing something, it's much easier to continue doing it. And if you get your foot in the door, you can eventually scale it into the habit that you want.

To practice, write out the ideal version of your habit and then brainstorm a few ways the two-minute version could look. The key to this is to think granularly. It can be scaling down the habit—reading one page instead of reading twenty—but it can also be accomplishing just the beginning of what you hope will become a longer habit: only putting on your workout clothes instead of actually going to the gym.

Habit: _____

Ideal Version	Two-Minute Version

Now choose one of those two-minute versions and try it for a week. Then come back here to reflect.

Reflection After One Week: How did it go? Were you able to stick with this version of the habit? Do you want to make any adjustments and try again?

_____

_____

_____

_____

↻ ···

Habit: _____

Ideal Version	Two-Minute Version

Now choose one of those two-minute versions and try it for a week. Then come back here to reflect.

Reflection After One Week: How did it go? Were you able to stick with this version of the habit? Do you want to make any adjustments and try again?

_____

_____

_____

_____

WHEN TO STOP

> *Do less than you're capable of, but do it more consistently than you have before.*

Even if you plan out the two-minute version of the habit, it can be difficult to actually stick with this easy version without letting yourself creep into a more difficult one. The Two-Minute Rule can feel like a ruse. Maybe you're telling yourself that since the goal is really to do the habit for longer, the two minutes is just a mental gimmick to get you in the door, after which you should actually keep going. The problem with this is that it reduces the power of the Two-Minute Rule, because it encourages you to progress too soon, making the habit difficult when the whole point is to make it effortless.

If this is the case for you, set an alarm for two minutes and when it goes off, no matter how much of the habit you have accomplished, cut yourself off. Always staying below the point where the habit feels like work ensures a positive feedback loop and increases the likelihood that you will actually perform it again.

SCALING A HABIT BY MAKING IT FUN

One specific way to scale a habit down to its easiest, most doable form is by simply making it fun. Identifying the fun version of your habit can help make your habit attractive and has the added benefit of making it feel easier too. If you're trying to start a workout routine but running feels like a chore, sign up for a dance class instead. Fun music, classmates, and a set start and stop time make it both easy to stick with and enjoyable.

Switching to a more fun version of your habit can be the entire strategy for behavior change. Or, as with the Two-Minute Rule, you can use the fun version to get you in the door, and then once that version feels locked in, scale up your habit to the ideal version you'd originally planned. Start with the dance class, and once you're in a rhythm of moving your body multiple times a week, swap out one of those classes for outdoor runs. Now that you're used to moving regularly and your cardio fitness is improved, running will likely feel less difficult and more pleasurable.

Below, write out the ideal version of your habit and then brainstorm what the fun versions of this habit would look like. The easier and more enjoyable it is, the more likely that you'll stick with it.

Habit: _____

Ideal Version	Fun Version

Now choose one fun version and try it for a week. Then come back here to reflect.

Reflection After One Week: How did it go? Were you able to stick with this version of the habit? Do you want to make any adjustments and try again?

_____

_____

_____

Habit: _____

Ideal Version	Fun Version

Now choose one fun version and try it for a week. Then come back here to reflect.

Reflection After One Week: How did it go? Were you able to stick with this version of the habit? Do you want to make any adjustments and try again?

_____

_____

_____

It's rarely doing the work that is hard; it's starting the work. Once you begin, it's often less painful to continue working. This is why—in the beginning—it is often more important to build the habit of getting started than it is to worry about whether or not you are doing enough.

Reflect on this quote. How does it apply to your life and habits, and what can you learn from it?

_____

_____

_____

_____

_____

_____

_____

_____

HABIT SHAPING

While the easiest version of a habit is vital for getting you going, it is rarely the version of your habit you hope to be doing long term. If you've scaled back your exercise habit to just putting on your gym clothes, I'm willing to guess that you'd actually like to get to the gym one day! So how do you get from the easy version to the ideal version without accidentally making your habit too difficult again? The trick is a strategy called *habit shaping*.

With habit shaping, once you've mastered the two-minute version of the behavior, you scale it up ever so slightly, focusing on mastering that new level before scaling it up again. You repeat this process until you have reached the ideal version of the habit. The trick here is to *keep following the Third Law*. The key is to scale the habit while always staying at a level that feels easy. One way to do this is to move between levels using the same Two-Minute Rule. Whenever you level up your habit, always begin with the two-minute version of the new level so that it still feels easy.

RITUALIZING THE PROCESS

As you start scaling up your habit, the two-minute version of your habit doesn't disappear. Rather, it becomes the ritual that you always complete at the beginning of a larger routine, making it easier to slip into the mindset and focus needed for the full routine. This is part of the strategy behind warm-ups for athletes and musicians, or always setting up your desk the same way before you write. Your start-up ritual becomes a signal to yourself, helping you get in the headspace needed for the activity.

In order to practice habit shaping, you need to plan out the stages of the habit between the easiest and the ideal versions.

Below, for your habit, start by filling in "Phase 1" with the easy version you've been practicing, and then write the ideal version in "Phase 5." Then fill in the other phases with the steps between those versions of your habit.

Here is an example of habit shaping:

Phase 1	Phase 2	Phase 3	Phase 4	Phase 5
Change into workout clothes.	*Step out the door (try taking a walk).*	*Drive to the gym, exercise for five minutes, and leave.*	*Exercise for fifteen minutes at least once per week.*	*Exercise three times per week.*

Habit: _____

Phase 1	Phase 2	Phase 3	Phase 4	Phase 5

⟳ ···

Habit: _____

Phase 1	Phase 2	Phase 3	Phase 4	Phase 5

MASTER THE DECISIVE MOMENTS

Finding the smallest, easiest version of your habits matters because it helps you get the foot in the door of your habits. It also matters because it is the key to making the most of decisive moments.

Every moment of your day, you are making decisions. What's important to know is that not all decisions are equal in their impact. Some decisions we make are minor, while others end up impacting the entire day. For instance, in my life, I find that each day after work there is a small moment that shapes the rest of my night. When my wife gets home from work, we either head to the gym or we sit on the couch and spend the rest of the evening watching TV. The decisive moment here—what we do when my wife gets home from work—ends up determining the entire evening, and is far more impactful on our days than other decisions we make. Make that one decision, and the rest fall into place like dominoes.

The point here is that small moments can have outsize impacts on the rest of your time. Habits are not the end point of good decisions; they're the entry point.

To harness the power of decisive moments and make them work for you, start by taking an inventory of your day in order to determine what your decisive moments are. For a week, notice what you do during the different parts of the day, and write down the moments when you are aware that making a decision—no matter how small—is having a large impact on which path your day takes.

	Morning	Afternoon	Evening
Monday			
Tuesday			

	Morning	Afternoon	Evening
Wednesday			
Thursday			
Friday			
Saturday			
Sunday			

After a week, look back at what you wrote to see if you notice any patterns. What do you think are the decisive moments in your day? What are the typical options on either side of those decisive moments?

_____

_____

_____

_____

_____

Now let's see how we can make it as easy as possible to choose the path that leads to your desired behavior. For each decisive moment that you identified, write out the options on either side of the decision tree, circle the option you would prefer to take, and then write out the two-minute version of that path. For instance, returning to the example from my evenings, the two-minute version of the gym path is putting on our workout clothes. Just doing that two-minute habit is usually enough to send us down the entire gym path instead of the TV path.

Decisive Moment	Options	Two-Minute Habit

Now choose one of those two-minute habits and, for a week, try it during the decisive moment in your day. Then come back to reflect.

Reflection After One Week: How did it go? Were you able to do the two-minute version of the path? Did you find that you chose the desired path more than you usually do? Do you want to make any adjustments and try again?

_____

_____

_____

_____

_____

THE POWER OF FRICTION

Before you try to increase your willpower, try to decrease the friction in your environment.

Now that we've talked about how to make a habit easy to *start*, let's talk about how to make it easier to *perform*. You won't be surprised to hear that, just as with the First and Second Laws, the answer lies in your environment.

You can design your environment to influence the ease with which habits are performed. The key word here is *friction*, or how easy or difficult your environment makes it to perform your habit. For instance, consider your kitchen. What is on the highest shelf of the most difficult-to-reach cabinet? Whatever is placed there has a high degree of friction required to reach it, which means that a lot of energy is required to use those items (getting a step stool, or climbing on the counter). Now consider the things that are just out on the counter. These things have a very low degree of friction involved in accessing them, which means that they require almost no energy to reach. The result is that it's unlikely you will use the things on the high shelves and very likely you will use the things on the counter.

What's important is making sure that you're using this lever to your advantage. If you want to make more smoothies but your blender is on that highest shelf, it will be hard to build this habit. Conversely, if you're trying to drink less coffee but your coffee maker and beans are right on the counter, control will be more difficult.

The same is true for all environments you spend time in. Design them to facilitate the behaviors you want, and you will find that those behaviors feel like a breeze. Design them to make it difficult to perform the behaviors you don't want, and you will find it much easier to avoid those behaviors.

ENVIRONMENTAL ASSESSMENT

You know the drill. Before you start in on changing your environment, it's important to assess your current one.

To begin, go to a space in your house where you spend a lot of time and then look around. Notice what requires a lot of energy to do in that space (high friction) and what doesn't (low friction). Note that unlike with cues, this isn't necessarily about what's visible. Rather, when thinking about friction, this usually has more to do with what's easy to access and what's not.

Below, write out what habits this space facilitates and what habits it doesn't, and what makes these behaviors low or high friction.

Habits Facilitated	What Makes Them Low Friction	Habits Not Facilitated	What Makes Them High Friction

Now repeat this exercise in other rooms in your house in which you spend a significant amount of time or that your relevant habits occur in. You can also use this to evaluate relevant spaces outside your home, such as your office.

Space: _____

Habits Facilitated	What Makes Them Low Friction	Habits Not Facilitated	What Makes Them High Friction

Space: _____

Habits Facilitated	What Makes Them Low Friction	Habits Not Facilitated	What Makes Them High Friction

Space: _____

Habits Facilitated	What Makes Them Low Friction	Habits Not Facilitated	What Makes Them High Friction

Space: _____

Habits Facilitated	What Makes Them Low Friction	Habits Not Facilitated	What Makes Them High Friction

One additional space that is incredibly impactful on all our lives is the digital space—in particular, our phones and computers. Take a moment to repeat the activity for your digital space, noticing what your devices facilitate and what they don't.

Space: _____

Habits Facilitated	What Makes Them Low Friction	Habits Not Facilitated	What Makes Them High Friction

Now take a look at the assessment you've done of your spaces. What are you noticing? What patterns are you seeing in how your spaces are or aren't supporting your habits?

_____

_____

_____

_____

_____

_____

Based on your assessment, which spaces feel the most conducive to your habits, and which feel the least?

_____

_____

_____

_____

_____

_____

List some ideas for how you want to change those spaces to better support your habits:

_____

_____

_____

_____

_____

Take a moment to think in particular about your digital spaces. How are those spaces facilitating or not facilitating the habits you want? Do you have ideas for changes you could make to better support your habits?

_____

_____

_____

_____

_____

_____

DESIGNING YOUR ENVIRONMENT TO FACILITATE HABITS

Now that you've assessed your spaces, let's use the Third Law to design your environment for success.

Using your assessment, identify the environment most relevant to the habit you're working on building or breaking. Note that the environment might be digital.

Habit: _____ Environment: _____

Next, identify the things involved in this habit and how much friction there currently is around those objects in your environment. Then, in the right-most column, draw an arrow to indicate whether you want the degree of friction to move up or down for each item.

Item	Degree of Friction	↑↓

Based on your analysis above, brainstorm ways you could redesign your environment to facilitate your desired behavior. Note that the more achievable these ideas are, the more likely it is that you'll do them. For instance, while renovating your home to include an in-home gym would likely help facilitate an exercise routine, so might moving your yoga mat so that it's next to your couch.

_____

_____

_____

_____

_____

_____

Now implement the ideas you brainstormed, live with them for a week, and then return here to reflect on how it went.

Reflection After One Week: What was the most helpful? Which had the greatest impact on your target behavior? Does anything else need to be changed in your environment to facilitate your behavior change?

_____

_____

_____

_____

_____

Using your assessment, identify the environment most relevant to the habit you're working on building or breaking. Note that the environment might be digital.

Habit: _____ Environment: _____

Next, identify the things involved in this habit and how much friction there currently is around those objects in your environment. Then, in the right-most column, draw an arrow to indicate whether you want the degree of friction to move up or down for each item.

Item	Degree of Friction	↑↓

Based on your analysis above, brainstorm ways you could redesign your environment to facilitate your desired behavior. Note that the more achievable these ideas are, the more likely it is that you'll do them. For instance, while renovating your home to include an in-home gym would likely help facilitate an exercise routine, so might moving your yoga mat so that it's next to your couch.

_____

_____

_____

_____

_____

_____

Now implement the ideas you brainstormed, live with them for a week, and then return here to reflect on how it went.

Reflection After One Week: What was the most helpful? Which had the greatest impact on your target behavior? Does anything else need to be changed in your environment to facilitate your behavior change?

_____

_____

_____

_____

_____

_____

PRIME YOUR ENVIRONMENT FOR FUTURE BEHAVIORS

One specific form of environmental design that can help support your target behaviors is priming your environment. If you're trying to get in the habit of running in the morning, laying out your workout clothes and running shoes the night before can get you up and moving. And if you're trying to eat more home-cooked meals, meal prepping over the weekend might make weeknight cooking a breeze.

For your target habit, brainstorm if there are any ways you could prime your environment to help yourself perform your desired behaviors in the future.

Ways to Prime Your Environment
for Future Use:

_____

Habit:

_____

_____

_____

_____

_____

Now try implementing some for a week and then reflect on how it went.

Reflection After One Week: What was the most helpful? Did any of these succeed in helping you perform your habit in the future? Does anything else need to be changed in your environment to facilitate your future behaviors?

_____

_____

_____

_____

_____

_____

For your target habit, brainstorm if there are any ways you could prime your environment to help yourself perform your desired behaviors in the future.

Ways to Prime Your Environment
for Future Use:

_____

_____

Habit:

_____

_____

_____

_____

Now try implementing some for a week and then reflect on how it went.

Reflection After One Week: What was the most helpful? Did any of these succeed in helping you perform your habit in the future? Does anything else need to be changed in your environment to facilitate your future behaviors?

_____

_____

_____

MAKE IT HARD TO MESS UP

Your habits are often a byproduct of convenience. Humans are wired to seek the path of least resistance, which means the most convenient option is often the one that wins. Make good choices more convenient and bad choices less so. Behavior will improve naturally.

The Inverted First Law of Behavior Change is *make it difficult*. To stop yourself from performing a certain behavior, make it difficult to do the behavior. It's intuitive how this principle can be used for breaking habits— to break a habit, make it difficult to perform that habit—but it can be used for building habits as well: To build a habit, make it difficult to do anything except that habit. The next few exercises will play with this principle of how you can use ease and difficulty to make it impossible to do anything other than your desired behavior.

USE A COMMITMENT-KEEPING DEVICE

The first tool we'll work with is a *commitment-keeping device*, or a choice you make in the present that controls your actions in the future. Commitment-keeping devices lock in future behavior by limiting your ability to make future choices that could influence your behavior, thereby binding you to good ones and restricting you from bad ones.

For instance, if you want to work without the distraction of social media for a few hours, download software that prevents you from accessing certain websites for a set amount of time. Or if you want to learn a new skill but are struggling to find the time for it, sign up and pay for a class ahead of time.

Commitment-keeping devices are useful because they enable you to take advantage of good intentions before you can fall victim to temptation. They allow you to make a decision *for* your future self, making it so that future you must follow your desired behavior. The key is to make it so that it requires a lot more work *not* to do the desired behavior in the future than to follow through with it.

For the habit you are working on, brainstorm ways that you could employ commitment-keeping devices to help lock in your desired behavior.

Commitment-Keeping Devices:

_____

Habit: _____

_____   _____

_____

_____

Now choose one idea, try implementing it for a week, and then reflect on how it went.

Reflection After One Week: Was this helpful? Did you find that it successfully locked in your behavior? Do you want to tweak the device in any way or choose another one to try for a week?

_____

_____

_____

_____

_____

_____

_____

⟳ ....

For the habit you are working on, brainstorm ways that you could employ commitment-keeping devices to help lock in your desired behavior.

Commitment-Keeping Devices:

_____

Habit:

_____

_____

_____

_____

_____

Now choose one idea, try implementing it for a week, and then reflect on how it went.

Reflection After One Week: Was this helpful? Did you find that it successfully locked in your behavior? Do you want to tweak the device in any way or choose another one to try for a week?

_____

_____

_____

_____

AUTOMATE YOUR HABITS

Commitment-keeping devices aren't the only way to make decisions for your future self. You can go a step further by finding ways to automate your behaviors for the long term, so that only good behavior is available to you. As with commitment-keeping devices, automation enables you to make decisions while your motivation is high, taking your future decisions out of the equation. When working in your favor, automation can make your good habits inevitable

When you automate as much of your life as possible, you can spend your effort on the tasks machines cannot do yet.

and your bad habits impossible. But unlike with commitment-keeping devices, which usually work for only a specific time frame, automating good behavior means it can run on its own indefinitely. Automation is the ultimate way to lock in future behavior, rather than relying on willpower in the moment.

Automation can take many forms, but the most common involve technology. Setting up bills on auto-pay, automatically putting a portion of your paycheck into a retirement savings account, and using grocery subscription services are all ways that you can make good decisions automatic in the future.

Can you think of ways to automate any of the habits that you're working on? Automation isn't always applicable to or available for our daily habits, but if you think it could help, brainstorm on the next page.

Automation:

Habit:

_____

_____

_____

_____

_____

_____

Choose one automation idea, try implementing it for a week, and then reflect on how it went.

Reflection After One Week: Was this helpful? Did you find that it successfully locked in your behavior? Do you want to change the automation in any way or choose another one to try for a week?

_____

_____

_____

_____

_____

While automation is powerful, it is often the most useful when employed not for our daily habits, but for the behaviors that happen too infrequently to become habits. Behaviors that need to be done monthly or yearly—scheduling annual check-ups, remembering friends' birthdays, refilling prescriptions—will never be repeated frequently enough that they become habit. This leaves them at the mercy of memory and motivation, two incredibly fickle things. For these kinds of tasks, using automation can be a game changer.

While it may not be directly related to the primary behavior change you've been working on, employing automation can be an incredible tool to help you perform other behaviors and free up time and energy that you can then devote to the primary behavior change you are working on.

Can you think of behaviors in your life that could benefit from automation?

Below, brainstorm behaviors and ideas you have for how to automate them.

Behavior	Automation

ONETIME ACTIONS

In our efforts to make good behavior easy and bad behavior impossible, we can even go one step further. The most powerful version of automation goes beyond setting up a system that runs for you in the background: it's onetime actions that determine all behavior going forward.

Here are some examples of onetime actions that pay off in the long term. You'll notice that a number of them entail removing or canceling something you aren't using. The onetime action of definitively saying no to something means that you don't have to keep making the choice to not use the unwanted thing going forward.

Nutrition	Happiness
▪ Get Tupperware so that it's easy to bring home-cooked meals to work ▪ Get a water filter for your drinking water	▪ Live nearer to friends or family ▪ Put a piece of art that you love on your wall
Sleep	**General Health**
▪ Buy an eye mask ▪ Get a white-noise machine ▪ Move your alarm clock across the room so you have to get out of bed to turn it off	▪ Get vaccinated ▪ Make sure your desk setup is ergonomic ▪ Buy a gym membership ▪ Get an air filter for your house
Productivity	**Finance**
▪ Remove games and social media apps from your phone ▪ Have a friend change your password on social media sites so that you can't access them ▪ Set up a charging station for your phone that's out of sight so it won't distract you	▪ Cancel subscriptions you don't actively use ▪ Get a coffee machine instead of buying coffee out ▪ Invest in an index fund

Can you brainstorm other onetime actions you could take that could be beneficial to you? These might relate to the habits you're working on, but they don't have to.

- _____

- _____

- _____

- _____

- _____

- _____

CONCLUSION: THE THIRD LAW OF BEHAVIOR CHANGE

Now it's your turn. Based on what you've learned through these exercises, list out how you're going to use the Third Law of Behavior Change to influence the ease of implementing your habits. Think about what's worked for you and what hasn't, and feel free to combine principles in new ways. The goal is not to follow a template, but rather to experiment and find what works for *you*.

Habit: _____

How Will You Use the Third Law to Support Your Behavior Change?

Habit: _____

How Will You Use the Third Law to Support Your Behavior Change?

Look at what you've written and make a commitment to implement these strategies. These will be crucial as we move forward with the final law of behavior change.

CHEAT SHEET: THE THIRD LAW OF BEHAVIOR CHANGE

*The Third Law of Behavior Change is **Make It Easy.***
To build a habit, make it easy.

Key Principles	Exercises
Standardize First, Optimize Later ■ Focus on the doable version of your habit instead of the ideal version ■ Start small to make habits easy and reinforce your desired identity ■ Just starting is more important than being perfect	■ Use the Two-Minute Rule ■ Do the fun version of your habit ■ Start small, then scale up your habit
Master Decisive Moments ■ Certain moments in our days are more impactful than others	■ Master the decisive moment. Optimize the small choices that deliver outsize impact.
Design Your Environment ■ Reduce friction around good habits	■ Design your environment to make good habits easy
Lock In Future Behavior ■ Make decisions for your future self that make good behavior automatic	■ Use commitment-keeping devices ■ Use automation to make good behavior possible ■ Use onetime actions to make good behavior inevitable

*The Inverted Third Law of Behavior Change is **Make It Difficult.***
To break a habit, make it difficult.

Key Principles	Exercises
Master Decisive Moments ■ Certain moments in our days are more impactful than others	■ Master the decisive moment. Optimize the small choices that deliver outsize impact.
Design Your Environment ■ Increase friction around bad habits	■ Design your environment to make bad habits difficult
Lock In Future Behavior ■ Make decisions for your future self that make bad behavior impossible ■ Have it take more effort in the future to make the wrong choice	■ Use commitment-keeping devices ■ Use automation to make bad behavior impossible ■ Use onetime actions to make bad behavior impossible

CHECK-IN

Good choices create opportunities. Good habits
make the most of them.

How are things going so far?

_____

_____

_____

_____

How would you rate your overall progress?

    1   2   3   4   5   6   7   8   9   10

Are your habits continuing to reinforce the identity that you want to build?

_____

_____

_____

_____

What is at least one tiny victory from your work so far?

_____

_____

_____

What's working well? What's not?

_____

_____

_____

What obstacles are holding you back? How can you plan to overcome them?

_____

_____

_____

What have you learned?

_____

_____

_____

All big things come from small beginnings.

The seed of every habit is a single, tiny decision.

THE FOURTH LAW:
Make It Satisfying

ONCE A HABIT has been cued, a craving provoked, and a response performed, the final step in the habit loop is the reward—the outcome we receive from doing the habit. Specifically, it's how we *feel* at the end of the behavior. It's the delight at the taste of the potato chip or the pain from touching the hot stove, and it's the feedback that tells us whether we should repeat the behavior in the future. When a behavior results in a pleasurable outcome—a reward—we learn that it's one worth remembering and repeating. And when a behavior results in a negative outcome—a punishment—we learn that there is little reason to repeat it.

CUE   CRAVING

1 2
4 3

REWARD   RESPONSE

This is the foundation for the Cardinal Rule of Behavior Change: *What is rewarded is repeated. What is punished is avoided.* You learn what to do in the future based on what you were rewarded or punished for doing in the past. Positive emotions cultivate habits. Negative emotions destroy them.

There is one important caveat here: Because the human brain is hardwired for instant gratification, it's specifically the emotions *immediately* following the behavior,

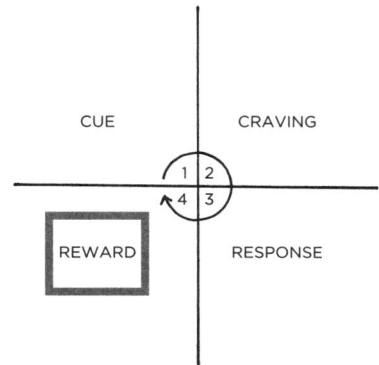

not the feelings of long-term satisfaction or disappointment, that are most impactful. This might seem like an easy tweak, but this small addition is at the root of why this principle can be so difficult to implement. The issue is that for good habits, while the long-term outcome feels good, the immediate outcome is usually unenjoyable. Whereas for bad habits, while the long-term outcome may feel bad, the immediate outcome frequently feels good. In other words, the costs of our good habits are in the present, while the costs of our bad habits are in the future, which is the inverse of what we need for positive behavior change. For this reason, making sure our good habits are immediately rewarded and our bad habits are immediately punished takes some creativity.

The Fourth Law of Behavior Change—*make it satisfying*—tells us how to use this lever to influence our habits. To build a habit, *make it satisfying*, and to break one, *make it unsatisfying*. If the first three laws of behavior change increase the likelihood that a behavior will be performed *this* time, the Fourth Law increases the likelihood that a behavior will be repeated *next* time and will transition from being a onetime action to a fully ingrained habit.

In the rest of this section, we will explore practical strategies to use the Fourth Law and its inverse to build and break habits. For the following exercises, you can use the habit(s) that you selected in Part I, or you can select new habits to focus on.

The Fourth Law of Behavior Change:
To build a habit, make it satisfying.
The Inverted Fourth Law of Behavior Change:
To break a habit, make it unsatisfying.

REINFORCEMENT

If the outcomes of our good habits are often naturally unsatisfying and those of our bad habits are naturally satisfying, how do we go about flipping them? The trick is to employ strategies that change the way the end of a habit *feels*, since what we're really talking about is whether the *end* of the behavior is satisfying or not.

In order to make the end of our good habits feel satisfying, we can use the strategy of *reinforcement*. Reinforcement is the act of linking the end of your behavior to an immediate reward. This makes your good behavior satisfying, even if it doesn't naturally have an immediate reward built in. For instance, say you are trying to develop the habit of meditating more. The problem is that at the beginning of this practice, meditation will be difficult and unsatisfying. The benefits you are looking for—feelings of peace, calm, and clarity—won't come until much later in the practice. Your task, therefore, is to make those early days of meditating still feel satisfying. Using reinforcement to do that means rewarding yourself, even in a small way, every time you meditate.

There are a number of ways to do this. One strategy is to use a financial reward, transferring five dollars into a savings account every time you perform the habit and getting the satisfaction of watching it build. Other rewards may be a cup of tea, a bubble bath, or listening to a song you like. A word of caution: It's important not to reward yourself with a behavior that counters the good behavior (for example, "If I don't go on social media for an hour, I'll reward myself by scrolling for a few minutes after"), as this can result in inadvertently rewarding the behavior you're trying to break.

Below, for the habit that you're working on, brainstorm ways you could use reinforcement to reward good behavior:

Ideas for Immediate Rewards:

_____

Habit:

_____

_____

_____

_____

_____

Now choose one reward you brainstormed and try implementing it for a week.

Reflection After One Week: How did it go? Did adding a reward help reinforce your habit? Do you need to tweak anything about your reward or select a new one and try again?

_____

_____

_____

_____

↻ ....

Below, for the habit that you're working on, brainstorm ways you could use reinforcement to reward good behavior:

Ideas for Immediate Rewards:

_____

Habit:

_____

_____

_____

_____

Now choose one reward you brainstormed and try implementing it for a week.

Reflection After One Week: How did it go? Did adding a reward help reinforce your habit? Do you need to tweak anything about your reward or select a new one and try again?

_____

_____

_____

REINFORCING BEHAVIORS OF AVOIDANCE

Reinforcement can be especially powerful when it comes to rewarding yourself for avoiding bad behavior, since this kind of behavior change can be extremely unsatisfying. For instance, if you're trying to stop buying so much coffee out, while the long-term benefit is obvious, it can be difficult to form positive associations with this behavior, since the act of not purchasing coffee is so anticlimactic. There is no immediate satisfaction that goes along with it.

In these cases, the goal is to make the benefits of avoiding the bad behavior visible and pleasurable, so it can feel satisfying. For example, if you're trying to stop going on social media, reinforce avoiding bad behavior by listening to a favorite song every time you successfully resist the urge to scroll.

Below, for the habit that you're working on, brainstorm ways you could use reinforcement to reward avoiding bad behavior.

Ideas for Immediate Rewards:

_____

Habit:

_____

_____

_____

_____

Now choose one reward you brainstormed and try implementing it for a week.

Reflection After One Week: How did it go? Did adding a reward help you avoid bad behavior? Do you need to tweak anything about your reward or select a new one and try again?

_____

_____

_____

_____

Below, for the habit that you're working on, brainstorm ways you could use rein-forcement to reward avoiding bad behavior.

Ideas for Immediate Rewards:

_____

Habit:

_____

_____

_____

_____

_____

Now choose one reward you brainstormed and try implementing it for a week.

Reflection After One Week: How did it go? Did adding a reward help you avoid bad behavior? Do you need to tweak anything about your reward or select a new one and try again?

_____

_____

_____

_____

TRACKING HABITS

One potent yet incredibly simple way to reinforce your habits is *habit tracking*, or the practice of making your progress visible. Making progress is inherently satisfying because it provides evidence that even if you haven't reached your goal yet, you're on the right path. The problem is that progress is often invisible, which limits its ability to feel like a reward. But by making progress visible, you can add a little satisfaction to any activity.

Tracking your habits can take many forms, but the best are visual. Checking off items on a to-do list is a version of this that many of us already employ. Another is to make a physical tracker, such as adding a coin or paper clip to a jar every time you complete an activity. Logging your behaviors—such as in a workout log or reading journal—can also work well. Many apps, like hydration logs and productivity timers, are also designed to make progress visible. And note that habit tracking can be used with equal effectiveness for building and breaking habits, since you can track behaviors you perform as well as ones you successfully avoid.

MEASURE THE RIGHT THING

Remember to make sure you're avoiding the pitfall of measuring the wrong thing. We often seek to build habits in order to make meaningful change, but habit tracking can lead us down the path of prioritizing completion over whether the habit is actually having the impact we want it to. For instance, if you want to read more, you might think it's a good idea to track the number of books you read annually, aiming for a higher number each year. However, this can easily result in you prioritizing short, easy books that don't feel meaningful to you, purely so that you can hit your reading goal. While this will result in you reaching your goal, it might also strip the habit of the significance you were hoping it would provide in the first place.

So as you track your habits, make sure that you're tracking the right thing and that tracking is the right strategy for you. It might not be!

Below, for the habit you're working on, design a tracker or two that you could use to make your progress visible. What would it look like? Is it visual or physical? Does it use technology or employ an app? Then use your system to track your habit for one week.

Habit: _____

Tracker Idea 1	Tracker Idea 2

Reflection After One Week: How did it go? Did tracking your habit make it feel more satisfying? Did it help you stick with it? Do you need to change anything about your system and try again?

_____

_____

_____

_____

Below, for the habit you're working on, design a tracker or two that you could use to make your progress visible. What would it look like? Is it visual or physical? Does it use technology or employ an app? Then use your system to track your habit for one week.

Habit: _____

Tracker Idea 1	Tracker Idea 2

Reflection After One Week: How did it go? Did tracking your habit make it feel more satisfying? Did it help you stick with it? Do you need to change anything about your system and try again?

_____

_____

_____

_____

USE A HABIT TRACKER

A habit tracker is simple and usually takes the form of a calendar where you note every day that you successfully perform the habit you're trying to build or avoid the habit you're trying to break. Over time, you can see how often you performed the habit, and how consistently. The drive to never miss a day is a powerful one, and can motivate you to make sure that you do what needs to be done so that you have a neat, unbroken chain of Xs. Here is an example of a habit tracker:

	Monday	Tuesday	Wednesday	Thursday	Friday	Saturday	Sunday
Floss	X	X	X	X	X	X	X
Meditate				X	X	X	X

But beware all-or-nothing thinking. It's easy for the desire to never miss to result in you giving up on your habit entirely as soon as you break the streak. This is a problem because it is inevitable that sometimes you're going to miss. You go on vacation, you have a hard day, life is too busy—these things happen. The problem is not slipping up; the problem is thinking that if you can't do something perfectly, then you shouldn't do it at all. In order to not let yourself be derailed by perfectionism, use the mantra *Never miss twice*.

THE "NEVER MISS TWICE" TRACKER

In order to make a habit tracker that focuses on never missing twice, use two different color pens to fill it out. Put a green dot on days when you perform the habit, and put a red dot on days when you don't. Seeing the red dot will be a powerful visual cue to not miss again, and the goal will be to never have two red dots in a row.

The first mistake is never the one that ruins you and it shouldn't be treated as such. What's important is that when you do make a mistake, you course correct and get right back on track, so that missing doesn't become the new habit. This is why the days when you do a habit imperfectly can be the most important ones. Having a "bad" workout, reading ten pages instead of twenty, or practicing guitar for just five minutes helps you still show up for your habit, reinforcing it so that you don't fall off course.

One nice thing about a habit tracker is that you can use it to track a number of things at once, a few habits at the same time, or another variable along with your habit. For instance, if you are trying to break the habit of scrolling on your phone and have an inkling that your scrolling might be related to your level of anxiety, you could track both whether you perform the habit and what your daily anxiety levels are, giving you added information.

For a habit tracker that you can use for the habits you're working on, flip to page 284 at the end of the "Toolbox" section of this workbook.

The feeling of progress is one of the best feelings of all.

This is true even when progress is small.

ACCOUNTABILITY PARTNERS

If you can add a little reward to the end of your habits to make them more satisfying, the inverse is also true. By adding a little punishment to the end of habits you're trying to break, you can make them less satisfying, decreasing the likelihood that you will repeat them.

One way to do this is to get an accountability partner to report to about your progress with your habit. If you don't do the habit you said you were going to do, you'll have to tell them when you check in. Same goes if you slip up and do the habit you said you weren't going to do. An accountability partner helps make bad behavior less satisfying by adding social pressure to the equation. Humans are social creatures, and knowing that someone else is watching can be a powerful motivator when it comes to sticking with behaviors.

An accountability partner can be purely someone you report your behavior to, or it can be someone who is also attempting the same behavior. In these situations, you act as accountability partners for each other, and the motivation goes both ways. This kind of accountability partnership can also be helpful because it creates a built-in support system, providing you with someone you can discuss the project and its difficulties with.

Below, brainstorm accountability partners and how you could work together. Then choose one and try it out for a few weeks.

Habit: _____

Accountability Partner	How You Will Work Together

Reflection After One Week: How is it having an accountability partner? Is it helping you stay on track? Do you need to adjust anything about your partnership?

_____

_____

_____

_____

Below, brainstorm accountability partners and how you could work together. Then choose one and try it out for a few weeks.

Habit: _____

Accountability Partner	How You Will Work Together

Reflection After One Week: How is it having an accountability partner? Is it helping you stay on track? Do you need to adjust anything about your partnership?

_____

_____

_____

_____

HABIT CONTRACT

A habit contract is another way to add a penalty to bad behavior to make it less satisfying. Just as a contract binds you to certain rules using the threat of legal action, a habit contract is an agreement that binds you to a certain behavior. Instead of legal action, a habit contract specifies a punishment that will occur if you don't stick with the behavior. For example, if you're trying to drink more water, a habit contract might state that for every day that you don't meet your water goals, you will pay a friend five dollars. Or if you're trying to stop ordering so much takeout, the habit contract might state that every time you order takeout, you won't be able to play video games for the next week.

A habit contract can be something that you do by yourself, but a way to make it even more impactful is to incorporate an accountability partner, having them sign the contract as well. That way, failing to follow the contract will not only result in the stated punishment, it will also result in the social pressure that comes with having an accountability partner.

The goal of a habit contract is to make the consequences of bad behavior a little more unpleasant in the moment so that the behavior seems less desirable. This strategy can be used to punish doing bad habits as well as failing to perform good habits, which means that it can be a useful tool no matter if you're trying to build or break habits.

To create your own habit contract, fill out the template on the next page for the habit you're working on.

Habit Contract

What is your main objective?

_____

If you don't follow through, what will be the consequence?

_____

Whom will you report to?

_____

Your Signature   Date

_____   _____

Accountability Partner's Signature   Date

_____   _____

Habit Contract

What is your main objective?

_____

If you don't follow through, what will be the consequence?

_____

Whom will you report to?

_____

Your Signature   Date

_____   _____

Accountability Partner's Signature   Date

_____   _____

CONCLUSION: THE FOURTH LAW OF BEHAVIOR CHANGE

Now it's your turn. Based on what you've learned through these exercises, list out how you're going to use the Fourth Law of Behavior Change to influence the satisfactoriness of your habits. Think about what's worked for you and what hasn't, and feel free to combine principles in new ways. The goal is not to follow a template, but rather to experiment and find what works for *you*.

Habit: _____

How Will You Use the Fourth Law to Support Your Behavior Change?

Habit: _____

How Will You Use the Fourth Law to Support Your Behavior Change?

Look at what you've written and make a commitment to implement these strategies. You now have all the tools you need to make your behavior change stick.

CHEAT SHEET: THE FOURTH LAW OF BEHAVIOR CHANGE

The Fourth Law of Behavior Change is **Make It Satisfying.**
To build a habit, make it satisfying.

Key Principles	Exercises
Good Behavior's Costs Are in the Present, and Rewards Are in the Future	▪ Add immediate rewards to good behavior to make it more immediately pleasurable
Make Performing Good Behavior and Avoiding Bad Behavior Satisfying	▪ Use reinforcement to add immediate rewards to the end of performing good behavior or avoiding bad behavior ▪ Track habits to make progress satisfying
Never Miss Twice ▪ Avoid getting derailed by the perfectionism of all-or-nothing thinking	▪ Use a "never miss twice" tracker ▪ Try the mantra of *Never miss twice* instead of *Don't break the streak*

The Inverted Fourth Law of Behavior Change is **Make It Unsatisfying.**
To break a habit, make it unsatisfying.

Key Principles	Exercises
Bad Behavior's Costs Are in the Future and Rewards Are in the Present	▪ Add immediate punishment to bad behavior to make it more immediately undesirable
Make Bad Behavior Unsatisfying	▪ Add an immediate punishment to the end of bad behavior ▪ Get an accountability partner to make bad behavior socially unpleasant ▪ Create a habit contract to make the costs of bad behavior immediately painful

CHECK-IN

Do one thing well and watch it compound.

How are things going so far?

_____

_____

_____

_____

_____

How would you rate your overall progress?

1   2   3   4   5   6   7   8   9   10

Are your habits continuing to reinforce the identity that you want to build?

_____

_____

_____

_____

_____

What is at least one tiny victory from your work so far?

_____

_____

_____

What's working well? What's not?

_____

_____

_____

What obstacles are holding you back? How can you plan to overcome them?

_____

_____

_____

What have you learned?

_____

_____

_____

If you keep showing up, you'll almost certainly break through—but probably not in the way you expected or intended. You need enough persistence to keep working and enough flexibility to enjoy success when it comes in a different form than you imagined.

PART III

Living with Your Habits

Building a Mindset for Long-Term Success

We want solutions, but what we really need are attitudes.

You don't need an easier life, but rather an attitude of

perseverance. Attitude precedes outcome.

A Mindset for Habits That Stick

WE BEGAN OUR journey by talking about continuous improvement and the idea that the path to your goals is through consistent incremental change— getting just 1 percent better every day. And here at the conclusion of this workbook, now that we've discussed the strategies for actually making this change happen, I want to return to this principle. But this time, what I want to highlight in particular is that when it comes to compounding, power is a function of time. A 1 percent growth will compound into massive change, but only if you give it the time to do so. Getting 1 percent better every day for a few weeks will not result in significant change. That will come only if you stick with it for the long haul.

In other words, an unpracticed habit can't compound. Which is why the final crucial skill to develop is the ability to keep practicing your habits *for as long as possible*. The longer you can make a habit stick, the more powerful it becomes.

But sticking with behavior change can be extremely tough. We've all had the experience of building a new habit just to have it go by the wayside when circumstances change or at the first moment of failure.

So how do you go about making behavior change stick for the long term, even when the going gets tough? The answer lies in adopting a mindset that can help you navigate these obstacles so that your habits are resilient in the face of whatever life throws your way.

In this final section, we'll explore the five pillars of a resilient mindset and look at how adopting them can help you overcome some of the most common obstacles.

PRIORITIZE ACTION OVER PERFECTION

One of the most difficult aspects of making behavior change stick for the long term is embracing how important it is to be OK with imperfection, especially at the start. This seems counterintuitive—isn't the point of behavior change to do things better? If you start off performing new habits badly, won't you run the risk of developing bad behavior?

What these questions forget is that perfectionism is the absolute death knell for behavior change. If you wait to perform your habit until you can do it perfectly, you'll never start. And even if you do start, if you wait for a perfect day and perfect circumstances, it's unlikely that you'll ever get in the reps you need for it to become fully ingrained. Our lives are too unpredictable, too imperfect for that, and this line of thinking only leads to procrastination.

This is why one of the most important skills is learning how to just start. Even if you can't run the full mile, a step in the right direction will always get you farther than not moving.

> *An imperfect start can always be improved, but obsessing over a perfect plan will never take you anywhere on its own.*

One crucial thing that can help with this is remembering that you rarely need to perform the perfect version of a habit in order for it to have a positive benefit. Don't underestimate the value of doing a habit for even just five good minutes. Five good minutes of push-ups is a solid workout, of conversation can rekindle a relationship, of meditation can reset your mood, of writing can clarify an idea. In the long run, those five minutes add up, and at the end of a year, you'll always be happier if you performed those five minutes consistently than if you did nothing. Writing for three hours every morning may be an ideal habit, but if you write for just five minutes a day, you will still be most of the way to a book draft in a year. The only way to not make any progress is to delay starting until that perfect three-hour morning appears. It might never appear—don't let that stop you. This is why these imperfect days—the "bad workouts," the "short sessions"—can be the most important. They're the ones that actually keep you in the game.

Reflection Questions

Motivation often comes after starting, not before. Action produces momentum. Where do you need to take action?

_____

_____

_____

_____

If you are delaying starting something, do you really need to plan more, or is it simply a matter of doing the work?

_____

_____

_____

_____

_____

What are you putting off starting for fear that you aren't ready or that it will be imperfect? What will help you get started?

_____

_____

_____

_____

What do you wish you had already started? How can you start it today?

_____

_____

_____

_____

THINK LONG-TERM

Even if you know that you should be planning ahead and not expect quick results, it can be hard to really embrace the realities of long-term thinking. We accept that we won't see change after a few weeks, but we get discouraged when we still haven't achieved our goals after six months. We make future goals, but we think only five years in the future, not ten. The problem with this is that the distant future is where all the payoff is, where compounding truly turns into results.

> *Aim to be great in ten years. Build health habits today that lead to a great body in ten years. Build social habits today that lead to great relationships in ten years. Build learning habits today that lead to great knowledge in ten years. Long-term thinking is a secret weapon.*

And since very few people truly think long-term, the distant future is also your competitive edge. Most people can stick with their plans for a few months, but if you can stick with your plans for a few *years*, you'll be far ahead of the pack. Most people make a three-year plan, but if you can make a ten-year plan, you can achieve much more.

But long-term thinking only works if you pair it with short-term action. Planning for the future does nothing if you only ever lie in wait. Think long-term, but don't delay. Take consistent, daily actions that lead to long-term results.

> *Patience is a competitive advantage. In a surprising number of fields, you can find success if you are simply willing to do the reasonable thing longer than most people.*

Reflection Questions

What can you do in the next hour that will help you move toward where you want to be in ten years?

_____

_____

_____

_____

Where do you want to be in five years? Ten years? Twenty? When you're looking back at the end of your life?

_____

_____

_____

_____

_____

_____

When is it hardest for you to think long-term? What can you do to remind yourself of the bigger picture during those moments?

_____

_____

_____

_____

_____

_____

_____

_____

STAY FOCUSED

At some point in every project, there is a moment when motivation inevitably begins to fade. The excitement from the initial phase wears off, the end goal is still out of sight, and you feel your enthusiasm plateau. In that moment, it is the easiest thing in the world to let that loss of drive win, and more often than not, we do. The key to pushing through this plateau is to stay focused.

As obvious as it may seem, it's amazing how easy it is to lose sight of the big picture of what you're trying to achieve. Having a clear sense of where you are heading and what you are optimizing for can help you stay the course and not stray from your plan, even when the going gets tough. Always remember what you're working toward and why. A strong sense of purpose can get you through even the toughest plateau.

Focus also gives you an edge in a world of distractions. Our time is finite, and letting our attention get pulled in too many directions only dilutes our ability to accomplish great things. So before you try working harder, staying up later, and spreading yourself thinner, try taking a moment to focus.

Before you throw more time at the problem, throw more focused action at the problem. It's possible that what you need isn't more time, but fewer distractions. Don't look for things to add. Look for things to eliminate.

Time is your greatest resource, and everything you can eliminate puts power back in your hands. When you say no, you are only saying no to one option. When you say yes, you are saying no to every other option. No is a decision. Yes is a responsibility. Say no to commitments and cut back on unnecessary tasks—spend your energy wisely.

Reflection Questions

How do you reconnect with your "why" when motivation naturally dips?

_____

_____

_____

_____

What is something that feels productive to you in the moment but usually ends up wasting time and energy?

_____

_____

_____

_____

_____

_____

What is taking up too much of your energy? What do you wish you could say no to right now?

_____

_____

_____

_____

_____

Momentum is a double-edged sword. It can propel you to new heights, or keep you locked into previous choices and old habits. Where do you have healthy momentum right now? Where do you have unhealthy momentum?

_____

_____

_____

_____

_____

PLAN FOR FAILURE AND RECOVER QUICKLY

It is also inevitable that from time to time you will experience setbacks. You won't achieve your goal, you will encounter an obstacle that feels impossible to overcome, you will make mistakes and find yourself far off track. In these moments, it can feel like the project is over, like there's no way back, like the only thing to do is give up. When this happens, how do you move forward? How do you pick yourself up and not let the setback win?

The answer lies in learning how to recover quickly. Mistakes are learning moments, not final judgments. It's crucial to remember that success isn't about avoiding mistakes but about how you respond to them. In fact, failure is essential to the process. If you aren't failing, you aren't taking big enough swings. Let your mistakes teach you, but don't let them stop you.

> *The secret to winning is learning how to lose. That is, learning to bounce back from failure and disappointment—undeterred—and continuing to steadily march toward your potential. Your response to failure determines your capacity for success.*

The real problem lies not in the setbacks but in the self-judgment that can come from them. This is the real danger, as self-criticism and loss of confidence are more harmful to your progress than any failure will ever be. If you stop believing in yourself, that's yet another hurdle that you'll need to overcome on your path to your goals. So when you fail, resist the negative self-talk. Instead, give yourself grace, and remember that your value is not linked to the success of your project. Forgive yourself, pick yourself up quickly, and try again.

> *Make a mistake?*
> *Release the guilt; remember the lesson.*

And as much as you can, make planning for failure part of your process. The more you can anticipate obstacles, the more you can ensure that you aren't caught by surprise when they do arise. Planning is the shortcut to reacting to obstacles the best that you can, and perhaps even to avoiding them. Correct your mistakes before they become your habits.

Never expect to fail, but always plan for it. The fastest way to get back on track is to have a plan for when you're off it.

Reflection Questions

What is the most likely cause of failure? Before it happens, how can you prevent it? If it happens, how can you recover?

_____

_____

_____

How do you currently respond to missing a day or having a setback? What would a more productive response look like?

_____

_____

_____

How can you distinguish between a temporary slip and giving up entirely?

_____

_____

_____

_____

ADAPT AND BE FLEXIBLE

We've been talking a lot about long-term thinking, about making plans. But plans have a problem—they don't always work. How many times have you made a meticulous plan that you're *sure* accounts for every possible issue, that takes change and obstacles into account, only to have it go awry when you hit a snag you didn't expect? As much as we'd like to believe that we can prepare for any future, life is unpredictable, and it is incredibly difficult to plan accurately.

In these moments of unexpected change, what matters most is how you react. You can stay stuck in the past, wishing things were different, or you can accept your new reality and adapt accordingly. In these moments, flexibility and adaptability—not relentlessness—are where your power lies. Instead of doubling down on the plan that isn't working, accept the situation and make the changes needed to move forward. Change is inevitable, and fighting it will only ever waste your energy.

This is also an important caveat to conversations about consistency and making sure your habits compound for the long term. In theory, consistency is about being disciplined, determined, and unwavering. In practice, consistency is about being adaptable. Don't have much time? Scale it down. Don't have much energy? Do the easy version. Find different ways to show up depending on the circumstances. Let your habits change shape to meet the demands of the day and

The ultimate form of preparation is not planning for a specific scenario, but a mindset that can handle uncertainty.

the season of your life. When change is necessary, it doesn't mean that you or your habits have failed. It just means that you're growing and that your habits have to grow with you.

Reflection Questions

What was a time when you had to be flexible and adapt? What was the outcome?

_____

_____

_____

_____

_____

What habit used to work for you but needs to change to fit your current life?

_____

_____

_____

_____

_____

What are the areas where you find it the most difficult to be flexible? What can you do to change that?

_____

_____

_____

_____

_____

_____

_____

CONTINUOUS REVIEW

One of the best ways to make sure that you're building an adaptable mindset, resilient to whatever life will throw your way, is to implement a process of reflection.

To do this, try implementing a frequent review process. This will not only help you take stock and make necessary changes, but it will also help you gain perspective and notice progress you may have failed to appreciate. Here is the simple semi-annual review process I use as a guide.

End-of-Year Review

1. Tally up your progress toward your habits:

_____

_____

_____

_____

_____

_____

_____

2. Reflect on your progress:

    a. What went well this year?

_____

_____

_____

_____

_____

    b. What didn't go so well this year?

_____

_____

_____

_____

c. What did you learn?

_____

_____

_____

_____

_____

Midyear Integrity Report

1. What are the core values that drive your life and work?

_____

_____

_____

_____

_____

_____

2. How are you living and working with integrity right now?

_____

_____

_____

_____

_____

3. How can you set a higher standard in the future?

_____

_____

_____

_____

_____

Win enough to keep progressing.

Lose enough to keep learning.

Toolbox

Your first task is to find what feels effortless to you.

Your second task is to put maximum effort into it.

Habit Shortlist

THE MOST POWERFUL IDEAS IN ONE PAGE

1 Percent Better Every Day: Success is the product of daily habits—not once-in-a-lifetime transformations. Focus on improving by just 1 percent every day, and you'll get thirty-seven times better in one year because of compounding.

Start with Identity: It's easiest to perform behaviors that align with your identity. Focus on who you want to be, not on what you want to achieve, and the behaviors will follow.

Focus on Systems, Not Goals: Goals are good for setting direction, but systems are necessary for getting there. Focus on creating the right system, and it will bring you to your goal.

CUE	→	CRAVING	→	RESPONSE	→	REWARD

To Build Habits

First Law *Make It Obvious*	Second Law *Make It Attractive*	Third Law *Make It Easy*	Fourth Law *Make It Satisfying*
■ Use habit stacking ■ Design environment to make cues obvious	■ Use temptation bundling ■ Redesign social environment to support habits	■ Use the Two-Minute Rule ■ Try the fun version of your habit ■ Design environment to reduce friction ■ Master decisive moments ■ Use commitment-keeping devices	■ Use reinforcement ■ Track your habits

To Break Habits

Inverted First Law *Make It Invisible*	Inv. Second Law *Make It Unattractive*	Inverted Third Law *Make It Difficult*	Inv. Fourth Law *Make It Unsatisfying*
■ Identify cues in order to eliminate them ■ Redesign physical environment to reduce cues	■ Identify cravings in order to eliminate them ■ Find better ways to address cravings ■ Design social environment to support habits ■ Reframe your mindset	■ Design environment to increase friction ■ Master decisive moments ■ Use commitment-keeping devices	■ Get an accountability partner ■ Create a habit contract

Navigate Obstacles with the Right Mindset

- ■ Prioritize action over perfection
- ■ Think long-term
- ■ Stay focused
- ■ Plan for failure and recover quickly
- ■ Adapt and be flexible
- ■ Review and make changes

Quick-Start Worksheet for Habit Building

BUILD A HABIT IN ONE PAGE

Habit You're Building:

_____

Identity That This Habit Supports:

_____

CONFIRM THAT YOU'RE FOCUSING ON A SYSTEM, NOT A GOAL ❑

Ways to Make the Habit Obvious	**Ways to Make the Habit Attractive**
Ways to Make the Habit Easy	**Ways to Make the Habit Satisfying**

PREPARE FOR SETBACKS

Potential Obstacles	**Plans to Overcome Them**

Quick-Start Worksheet for Habit Breaking

BREAK A HABIT IN ONE PAGE

Habit You're Breaking:

_____

Identity That Breaking This Habit Supports:

_____

CONFIRM THAT YOU'RE FOCUSING ON A SYSTEM, NOT A GOAL ❑

Ways to Make the Habit Invisible	**Ways to Make the Habit Unattractive**

Ways to Make the Habit Difficult	**Ways to Make the Habit Unsatisfying**

PREPARE FOR SETBACKS

Potential Obstacles	**Plan to Overcome Them**

Cheat Sheet: Building Good Habits

KEY PRINCIPLES	EXERCISES
*The First Law of Behavior Change is **Make It Obvious.*** *To build a habit, make it obvious.*	
Craft Strong, Obvious Cues ■ Build cues to trigger new habits. The more obvious the cue, the more likely it is to trigger the habit. ■ Use the five cue types: time, location, preceding events, emotions, other people ■ Pick cues that are specific and immediately actionable	■ Use implementation intentions: "I will [BEHAVIOR] at [TIME] in [LOCATION]" ■ Use habit stacking: "Before/After I [CURRENT HABIT], I will [NEW HABIT]" ○ Use single stacks, routine stacks, and larger stacks ■ Pointing-and-calling makes habits obvious

Design Your Environment
 ■ Behavior is a function of your environment
 ■ Design your environment to make your cues as obvious as possible
    ○ Cues can use any of your senses, but visual cues are the strongest
    ○ Sprinkle your environment with multiple cues
 ■ It can be easier to start a new habit in a new space
 ■ One space, one use
	■ Redesign your environment to make the cues of good habits obvious and visible
	 ■ Choose a new space to perform your new habit in
	 ■ Section off a space within your current environment

*The Second Law of Behavior Change is **Make It Attractive.*** *To build a habit, make it attractive.*	
Create Cravings ■ Habits are attractive when we associate them with positive feelings ■ New habits are not yet associated with positive feelings, so we need to *make* them something we crave	■ Use temptation bundling. Pair an action you *need* to do with an action you *want* to do. ■ Make your habits fun ■ Create a motivation ritual ■ Reframe your mindset. Highlight the benefits of performing your good habits.
Social Environment Design ■ Our social environment—groups we're a part of and relationships we're in—is the biggest determiner of the attractiveness of our habits	■ Design your social environment to support your changing habits ■ Join a culture where your desired behavior is the normal behavior

KEY PRINCIPLES	EXERCISES
*The Third Law of Behavior Change is **Make It Easy.*** *To build a habit, make it easy.*	
Standardize First, Optimize Later ▪ Focus on the doable version of your habit instead of the ideal version ▪ Start small to make habits easy and reinforce your desired identity ▪ Just starting is more important than being perfect	▪ Use the Two-Minute Rule ▪ Do the fun version of your habit ▪ Start small, then scale up your habit
Master Decisive Moments ▪ Certain moments in our days are more impactful than others	▪ Master the decisive moment. Optimize the small choices that deliver outsize impact.
Design Your Environment ▪ Reduce friction around good habits	▪ Design your environment to make good habits easy
Lock In Future Behavior ▪ Make decisions for your future self that make good behavior automatic	▪ Use commitment-keeping devices ▪ Use automation to make good behavior possible ▪ Use onetime actions to make good behavior inevitable
*The Fourth Law of Behavior Change is **Make It Satisfying.*** *To build a habit, make it satisfying.*	
Good Behavior's Costs Are in the Present, and Rewards Are in the Future	▪ Add immediate rewards to good behavior to make it more immediately pleasurable
Make Performing Good Behavior and Avoiding Bad Behavior Satisfying	▪ Use reinforcement to add immediate rewards to the end of performing good behavior or avoiding bad behavior ▪ Track habits to make progress satisfying ▪ Use a habit tracker to make progress satisfying
Never Miss Twice ▪ Avoid getting derailed by the perfectionism of all-or-nothing thinking	▪ Use a "never miss twice" tracker ▪ Try the mantra of *Never miss twice* instead of *Don't break the streak*

Cheat Sheet: Breaking Bad Habits

KEY PRINCIPLES	EXERCISES
The Inverted First Law of Behavior Change is **Make It Invisible.** *To break a habit, make it invisible.*	
Identify Your Cues and Make Them Invisible	■ Use pointing-and-calling to identify cues
Rewire the Cues of Bad Habits	■ Use habit stacking to rewire current cues
Design Your Environment ■ Behavior is a function of your environment ■ Design your environment to make your cues as invisible as possible	■ Redesign your environment to make the cues of bad habits invisible
Self-Control Is a Myth ■ The secret to self-control is to not have to use it ■ People who seem to have better self-control really just spend their time in less tempting situations	■ Instead of spending energy avoiding the temptation of bad habits, design your environment to reduce temptations as much as possible
The Inverted Second Law of Behavior Change is **Make It Unattractive.** *To break a habit, make it unattractive.*	
Identify Cravings ■ Identify why you crave your bad habits so that you can address these cravings ■ Habits are solutions to your cravings. If you identify your craving, you can find a better solution for it.	■ Use pointing-and-calling to notice your cravings as they occur ■ Find alternative habits to fit your cravings
Make Your Bad Habits Unattractive	■ Reframe your mindset. Highlight the benefits of avoiding your bad habits.
Social Environment Design ■ Our social environment—groups we're a part of and relationships we're in—is the biggest determiner of the attractiveness of our habits	■ Design your social environment to support your changing habits ■ Leave the groups that enable your bad habits, and join groups that support changing them

KEY PRINCIPLES	EXERCISES
The Inverted Third Law of Behavior Change is ***Make It Difficult.*** *To break a habit, make it difficult.*	
Master Decisive Moments ▪ Certain moments in our days are more impactful than others	▪ Master the decisive moment. Optimize the small choices that deliver outsize impact.
Design Your Environment ▪ Increase friction around bad habits	▪ Design your environment to make bad habits difficult
Lock In Future Behavior ▪ Make decisions for your future self that make bad behavior impossible ▪ Have it take more effort in the future to make the wrong choice	▪ Use commitment-keeping devices ▪ Use automation to make bad behavior impossible ▪ Use onetime actions to make bad behavior impossible
The Inverted Fourth Law of Behavior Change is ***Make It Unsatisfying.*** *To break a habit, make it unsatisfying.*	
Bad Behavior's Costs Are in the Future and Rewards Are in the Present	▪ Add immediate punishment to bad behavior to make it more immediately undesirable
Make Bad Behavior Unsatisfying	▪ Add an immediate punishment to the end of bad behavior ▪ Get an accountability partner to make bad behavior socially unpleasant ▪ Create a habit contract to make the costs of bad behavior immediately painful

Habit Tracker

	1	2	3	4	5	6	7	8	9	10	11	12	13
MONTH	JAN		FEB		MAR		APR			MAY		JUN	
HABIT													

If you want to make a "never miss twice" tracker, instead of checking off habits, use two pen colors, one to indicate you've done a habit and one to indicate you missed. Your goal is to never see two "misses" in a row.

14	15	16	17	18	19	20	21	22	23	24	25	26	27	28	29	30	31	
JULY			AUG			SEPT			OCT			NOV			DEC			TOTAL

Habit Tracker

MONTH			1	2	3	4	5	6	7	8	9	10	11	12	13
	JAN		FEB		MAR			APR			MAY			JUN	
HABIT															

If you want to make a "never miss twice" tracker, instead of checking off habits, use two pen colors, one to indicate you've done a habit and one to indicate you missed. Your goal is to never see two "misses" in a row.

14	15	16	17	18	19	20	21	22	23	24	25	26	27	28	29	30	31	
JULY			AUG			SEPT			OCT			NOV			DEC			TOTAL

Habit Tracker

	1	2	3	4	5	6	7	8	9	10	11	12	13
MONTH	JAN		FEB		MAR		APR		MAY		JUN		
HABIT													

If you want to make a "never miss twice" tracker, instead of checking off habits, use two pen colors, one to indicate you've done a habit and one to indicate you missed. Your goal is to never see two "misses" in a row.

14	15	16	17	18	19	20	21	22	23	24	25	26	27	28	29	30	31	
JULY			AUG			SEPT			OCT			NOV			DEC			TOTAL

Habit Tracker

		1	2	3	4	5	6	7	8	9	10	11	12	13
MONTH		JAN		FEB		MAR		APR		MAY		JUN		
HABIT														

If you want to make a "never miss twice" tracker, instead of checking off habits, use two pen colors, one to indicate you've done a habit and one to indicate you missed. Your goal is to never see two "misses" in a row.

14	15	16	17	18	19	20	21	22	23	24	25	26	27	28	29	30	31	
JULY			AUG			SEPT			OCT			NOV			DEC			TOTAL

Habit Tracker

		1	2	3	4	5	6	7	8	9	10	11	12	13
MONTH		JAN		FEB		MAR		APR		MAY		JUN		
HABIT														

If you want to make a "never miss twice" tracker, instead of checking off habits, use two pen colors, one to indicate you've done a habit and one to indicate you missed. Your goal is to never see two "misses" in a row.

14	15	16	17	18	19	20	21	22	23	24	25	26	27	28	29	30	31	
JULY			AUG			SEPT			OCT			NOV			DEC			TOTAL

Habit Tracker

	1	2	3	4	5	6	7	8	9	10	11	12	13
MONTH	JAN		FEB		MAR		APR		MAY		JUN		
HABIT													

If you want to make a "never miss twice" tracker, instead of checking off habits, use two pen colors, one to indicate you've done a habit and one to indicate you missed. Your goal is to never see two "misses" in a row.

14	15	16	17	18	19	20	21	22	23	24	25	26	27	28	29	30	31	
JULY			AUG			SEPT			OCT			NOV			DEC			TOTAL

Habit Tracker

	1	2	3	4	5	6	7	8	9	10	11	12	13
MONTH	JAN		FEB		MAR		APR		MAY			JUN	
HABIT													

If you want to make a "never miss twice" tracker, instead of checking off habits, use two pen colors, one to indicate you've done a habit and one to indicate you missed. Your goal is to never see two "misses" in a row.

14	15	16	17	18	19	20	21	22	23	24	25	26	27	28	29	30	31	
JULY			AUG			SEPT			OCT			NOV			DEC			TOTAL

Habit Tracker

MONTH		1	2	3	4	5	6	7	8	9	10	11	12	13
		JAN		FEB		MAR		APR		MAY		JUN		
HABIT														

If you want to make a "never miss twice" tracker, instead of checking off habits, use two pen colors, one to indicate you've done a habit and one to indicate you missed. Your goal is to never see two "misses" in a row.

14	15	16	17	18	19	20	21	22	23	24	25	26	27	28	29	30	31	
JULY			AUG			SEPT			OCT			NOV			DEC			TOTAL

Habit Tracker

		1	2	3	4	5	6	7	8	9	10	11	12	13
MONTH		JAN		FEB		MAR		APR		MAY		JUN		
HABIT														

If you want to make a "never miss twice" tracker, instead of checking off habits, use two pen colors, one to indicate you've done a habit and one to indicate you missed. Your goal is to never see two "misses" in a row.

14	15	16	17	18	19	20	21	22	23	24	25	26	27	28	29	30	31	
JULY			AUG			SEPT			OCT			NOV			DEC			TOTAL

Habit Tracker

	1	2	3	4	5	6	7	8	9	10	11	12	13
MONTH	JAN		FEB		MAR		APR		MAY		JUN		
HABIT													

If you want to make a "never miss twice" tracker, instead of checking off habits, use two pen colors, one to indicate you've done a habit and one to indicate you missed. Your goal is to never see two "misses" in a row.

14	15	16	17	18	19	20	21	22	23	24	25	26	27	28	29	30	31	
JULY			AUG			SEPT			OCT			NOV			DEC			TOTAL

Habit Tracker

		1	2	3	4	5	6	7	8	9	10	11	12	13
MONTH		JAN		FEB		MAR		APR		MAY		JUN		
HABIT														

If you want to make a "never miss twice" tracker, instead of checking off habits, use two pen colors, one to indicate you've done a habit and one to indicate you missed. Your goal is to never see two "misses" in a row.

14	15	16	17	18	19	20	21	22	23	24	25	26	27	28	29	30	31	
JULY			AUG			SEPT			OCT			NOV			DEC			TOTAL

Habit Tracker

		1	2	3	4	5	6	7	8	9	10	11	12	13
MONTH		JAN		FEB		MAR		APR		MAY		JUN		
HABIT														

If you want to make a "never miss twice" tracker, instead of checking off habits, use two pen colors, one to indicate you've done a habit and one to indicate you missed. Your goal is to never see two "misses" in a row.

14	15	16	17	18	19	20	21	22	23	24	25	26	27	28	29	30	31	
JULY			AUG			SEPT			OCT			NOV			DEC			TOTAL